Love Thy Body

REAL LIFE STORIES

Volume 2

Love Thy Body

REAL LIFE STORIES

Volume 2

Love Thy Body Project

First published in 2021 by Love Thy Body Project

© 2021 Laura Bland, Serena Novelli, Ana Bonasera

The right of Laura Bland, Serena Novelli and Ana Bonasera to be identified as authors of this Work has been asserted by them in accordance with sections 77 and 78 of the Copyright, Designs and Patents Act 1988

A CIP catalogue record for this book is available from the British Library

Cover design and typesetting by Fuzzy Flamingo
www.fuzzyflamingo.co.uk

I am in constant awe of the women that surround me, understanding that their past does not define them but can be a beacon of light towards their own self-love journey and for others. To all the women in LTBP you are truly inspirational, supportive and kind. I am truly honoured to be in your presence daily. To my good friends Samantha, Emma-Jane and Karen, thank you for always encouraging me to shine, you are my constants and I am truly blessed to have you in my life.

Love & happiness

Serena xx

This book I dedicate to you, yes YOU. I see you struggling, I see that you have experienced pain, and I see that you want to create change. I know that you may be scared of what the future holds, but you are stronger than you could possibly know. Keep looking forward.

Love Always

Laura xx

It is with all my love and gratitude that I dedicate this book to my mother, for the care and strength she has passed on to me to become a mother myself. I also dedicate this book to all mothers and encourage you to find your way back to you, take some time to put yourself first and reconnect with your body, mind and soul.

Love & gratitude,

Ana xx

Contents

Foreword

As children we grow up dreaming of how our life will be, as adults we envision what our future will hold, more often than not those dreams, those visions turn out somewhat different to what we expected. We are thrown challenges, curveballs and mountains to climb, they can bring us to our lowest of lows and highest of highs.

With *Love Thy Body Real Life Stories Volume 2* you will find yourself getting lost in some of these ladies' most vulnerable moments. There may be moments you shed a tear, laugh, feel angry, frustrated and overjoyed from the stories that are about to unfold. It takes a lot of strength to get through life and everything it throws at us but to then find the courage to share their most precious moments that have made them who they are today shows unbelievable bravery.

These stories are not just about them but they are about you too. We will all face adversities in life, no one will be the same to another, however we can find some comfort knowing that others have lived on after their challenges and we hope that by these ladies courageously putting their lives on paper that it will inspire you to face any hardships that may have been or that may come your way.

In a world that feels so chaotic and hopeless right now, we hope that this book can bring you some hope and empowerment to your own life. If you love this please share it in hope that it could bring some light to someone else's life and if you ever need a shoulder to cry on, our Love Thy Body Project community is always open.

Serena, Laura & Ana

From Self-destruction to Self-love

Abi Morgan

"Scabby Abi", "Flabby Abi"; the words of not only bullies but friends that had been goaded, resounded in my head. The tears were running down my cheeks whilst I pressed the sharp edge of my broken swan ornament into my arm.

Slice.

Slice.

Slice.

Praying the physical pain would distract me from the torture of what was going on in my head.

This was a typical scene for me in my teens – for some reason I was an easy target for the bullies. Never one of the 'popular' kids. I was fine not being popular, but I didn't understand why I was constantly picked on. I concluded that I must have asked for it in some way. I must have offended them. It was my fault, and they were getting me back: physically, verbally and emotionally.

I was a nothing. Nobody liked me. Nobody cared

for me – for God's sake they could even get my friends involved!

I was scared to go out for the whole of the summer holidays one year as I was ganged up on on the first day and beaten up. My parents didn't know what was going on; although they loved me, we never really had a close relationship and I found it very difficult to open up and talk to them.

I started torturing myself as a way to cope, along with writing poetry. I would walk down the old railway in the pitch black to the bridge over the river. I would climb my way over the pipes to the concrete support and sit with my legs over the water. This was my quiet space. I considered jumping many times just so I could end it all and stop the pain. Luckily, I always had my notebook with me, so instead I would write:

"The still calm waters lay beneath my feet,
Nothing but darkness all around.
The sky above like black velvet
Is suffocating me.
Death is nothing to fear,
We should greet it with open arms,
As a way of release …"

I developed physically quite young and suddenly boys were interested in me. Yes, I know now they were predominantly men and were only interested in one thing. At the time, though, I felt wanted, needed and loved, so took a dangerous path in allowing my body to be used and abused even more. Getting myself into situations that were impossible to back out of; well, at the time they seemed impossible as I feared what would happen to me. It was only as I got older that I realised I was being coerced into doing things I didn't want to.

No surprises I fell pregnant at fourteen. So little respect I had for myself that I very ashamedly say that I have no idea who the father was. My parents were not impressed or supportive and told me to have an abortion. I thought long and hard about it myself and realised that it was the best option. I was a child that couldn't even look after herself. Somehow word got round the school, which gave the bullies new fuel for their fire. I sank even further into myself and questioned myself even more – now I wasn't just a nobody, now I felt like I was a murderer. School certainly was not a fun place for me and were some of the worst years of my life.

I worked hard from the age of fifteen, getting whatever work I could in a small village around my GCSEs and A-levels. I threw myself into my work and schoolwork as it was the only way I could get through the day. I knew I wanted to get away as well and make a fresh start, so had to get an education.

Despite being allowed in the pub from sixteen, things changed when I hit eighteen and could drink alcohol – I had a new way to numb the pain and would get wasted pretty much every night. This left me more open and vulnerable to be taken advantage of. I'm not proud to say but I had a reputation. At the time I really didn't give a damn, I needed to be wanted, to feel loved and needed. So, I carried on disrespecting myself. I didn't know any other way. No one had ever shown me any reason to think differently about myself.

I met my ex-husband when I was eighteen. He needed looking after. I finally had something else to turn my attention to. Someone did actually need me. More fool me! Trust me when I say you can't change someone. Nine years I spent in a controlling relationship. Being told what I could wear, that I always had to make an effort and wear make-up and high heels. I wasn't allowed to wear trackies because I looked like a slob and it wasn't sexy. My drinking had stopped, luckily, as his increased and so did the violence, the bloody noses, the black eyes, the gambling, the being forced to perform sexual acts with him and others that I didn't want to. Why didn't I walk away? Because I was a bloomin' mug and he always came back with "I'm sorry, I didn't mean to, it won't happen again". All the while that I was focused on his behaviour and trying to help him, I didn't have to pay any attention to my own demons.

Eventually, enough was enough when he gambled all my wages away in one evening, I saw some sense and plucked up the courage to leave. I realised that I hadn't done it before because I feared being alone – WTF I would rather have been in a relationship like that than on my own?!? I really didn't have an ounce of self-respect!

Shit. I was on my own. Damaged goods. Useless. Worthless. Nobody. Scabby Abi. Flabby Abi. What the hell do I do now?

I threw myself into going to the gym – I believed that I needed to somehow improve how I looked if anyone was ever going to pay attention, so I wouldn't have to stay alone. I needed someone as a distraction because I didn't want to have to face my own fears.

I was adopted as a child and tracked down my biological parents who had separated. I had been invited to my father's daughter's wedding reception. It was there that I met my now husband. I was off my face, single and having a good time. We clicked instantly and have been together since we first met thirteen and a half years ago. He was the first person that had genuinely shown an interest in me for who I was. Yes, we met when I was dolled up to the nines, but after all crashing at the house, he still liked me the following morning – the morning after the night before! Smudged make-up, bed hair, trackies and the hangover from hell. But he didn't remark on it, turn away or laugh – he just accepted it for who I was. He didn't even take advantage of me in my drunken state and we didn't even sleep with each other for a while. He respected me. This was a huge turning point for me. The first ounce of self-respect gained. I finally realised that I may have some worth.

Eventually I fell pregnant. I had always thought I couldn't as I was twenty-nine and hadn't been on contraception for some time, even with my ex-husband (thank God that didn't happen). I thought the universe was punishing me for murdering my unborn child when I was younger. The year of my pregnancy was hell with lots of family illness and death. I even thought my husband was going to die in hospital with pneumonia. This triggered a premature birth at thirty weeks. I had failed at pregnancy. My body couldn't do what it was supposed to. To top it off I couldn't breastfeed. The two most natural things for a woman and me being as useless as I was couldn't do it. It was torture leaving my tiny 3lb 1oz baby in the hospital and I blamed myself. We were extremely lucky that he was relatively well and just needed to feed and grow. He came home six weeks later but my depression and anxiety had kicked in. *I don't deserve a child. I'm a crap mother. He would be better off without me.* But, suddenly, I wasn't as impulsive as before. I had this tiny baby that was dependent on me. I had already failed him, and I couldn't fail him anymore. So, I locked my feelings away. My husband's family were very close and supportive, but I didn't make an effort with myself. I was a mess and slobbed around in my maternity clothes. I'm a mum now, there's no time for me.

Six months later I was pregnant again. OMG "I'm a failure" masterclass! I developed SPD again, where my pubic bone separated too much and I could barely walk. My mother-in-law had to look after my eldest for six weeks because I was physically unable to, but this had to be at hers as she had dogs that needed looking after and didn't drive herself. I was failing my baby. How on earth was I going to cope with two under two? I had another early birth at thirty-six weeks; again, I couldn't breastfeed. Again, I blamed myself and my body. I was useless.

As the children grew older, I noticed something wasn't right with their behaviours and so started the long battle with the so called "professionals". I was useless at it. I had no spine. I spent years accepting them telling me it was my fault, it was my parenting, I was a bad parent. I was knocked down even further. The only snag is that now it was having an impact on my boy's future.

I discovered online networking and started to surround myself with positive people instead of using it to just moan and whinge. I started to understand where my insecurities and beliefs had come from and started to realise that I wasn't alone. I found supportive people and it was enlightening.

I fell pregnant again. Yes, he was early too at thirty-five weeks but for the first time I didn't blame myself or feel like a failure. I was able to breastfeed too because I was determined. I had researched and found loads of local support. I was confident enough to tell the midwives that the sensors don't work on me and had the best birth experience of all three. The other two were horrible but that's another story. I had started to find my voice and some confidence, and it felt great. Nearly two years I fed my youngest and was disappointed that no one confronted or challenged me as I was in a position to tell them what for. I had finally managed to succeed at something, my body wasn't failing and I sure as hell wasn't going to let anyone burst my bubble.

I found other groups online to join that were positive and supportive including 'Love Thy Body Project'. It's amazing the difference the right words can make and the way we speak to ourselves. I found my backbone to fight the "professionals" and go against what they were saying and weren't doing. I was finally confident enough in myself to stand up for my children. I was no longer failing them. It's still a journey we are on, but we are a lot further forward and I sure as hell won't be taking it lying down anymore. I know what's best for my children.

I found the courage to start my own business so I could work around my children's additional needs. I was putting myself out there on social media. Ridiculously I was able to be more myself when I had the security of a camera to hide behind. I started to realise that I had been missing out on so much by hating and denying myself for so long. Yes, I may not be the prettiest person in the world but who cares? I have other qualities and I was starting to discover them. I'm kind, caring and considerate to name a few!

I started to appreciate my body for what it had done instead of focus on what it hadn't. I started to realise that I could help others acknowledge this too and know they weren't alone. I started sharing positivity on Facebook. I encouraged people to be a part of the memory with their children and be in the picture with them. The child would remember the fun and laughter not whether you were wearing make-up or had a double chin. I was growing in my confidence every day; helped by helping others. Serena reached out and asked me to be a moderator for Love Thy Body Project. I questioned it, doubted myself and wondered why – that demon was still there. She explained that she had seen me growing and loved watching my journey. Don't get me wrong, I'm not completely there yet, but the power of being able to spread the message, encourage others and remind them they are not alone is incredible.

I downloaded audible and started listening to books on self-care and self-development whilst I was doing housework, etc. One thing that kept cropping up was limiting beliefs. Holding on to things from the past and not letting go of the fear – this is so true! I realised that I was letting what had happened all those years ago define me. I was a different person now and I needed new experiences to define me; more positive ones that showed me to the best of my ability.

I learnt about the Law of Attraction too. I have

always believed there was something out there, but I wasn't sure what – it is the universe! I started to practice gratitude and affirmations, setting my goals and keeping them in sight. It has worked absolute wonders for me this year. I love affirmations so much I was guided towards using them to help others and even do so in LTBP. I want to follow this up even more and learn the science behind it and help more people to positively change their mindset and see the best of themselves.

My husband regularly makes fleeting comments in jest and, although he means no malice, we have spoken about it because I want us to be more aware of the words and messages that we are passing on to our children, as I don't want them to battle the way I did. Children can be so unkind, and my boys are built like chalk and cheese, which makes for some very unkind name calling. Luckily, my middle son seems to have picked up the right mindset, telling me the other day that even though we are all different we are all beautiful. I was so pleased to hear him say this as he is a well-built young man entering puberty at the age of eight with additional needs in a special needs school, so is surrounded by other children that don't have any concept of the effect of what they are saying. My boy loves himself for who he is and that makes me so proud and inspires me to carry on and spread the message.

A few years back I got a tattoo on my arm that sums my journey up perfectly:

"I make mistakes and they make me."

Everything happened for a reason and I had to experience it to learn, grow and build from it to make me who I am now.

I still struggle from time to time and do take medication for my mental health because that is what works for me – trust me I know when I'm not taking it! So, don't be afraid to ask for additional help if you need it, there is no shame in it. I also have things about me that I don't like, the thinning hair on my head, and the excess hair on my body – particularly my chin, which got worse after each pregnancy. The difference now is that I accept they are part of me, and I have tools and coping methods to help me through. Plus, there are far more positive things about me that I learn to focus on.

That flabby, scabby Abi that was cutting her arms is now fierce and fabulous and shouting from the rooftops! Let go of your past. It doesn't define you. Don't let it eat you up and waste your life. Realise your worth because you are frickin' amazing! Xx

***

Abi is a part-time carer and has her own creations business. She lives in St Leonards, East Sussex with her husband, three boys and fur babies. She is passionate about helping people realise their worth and improving the confidence of future generations.

One of her favourite ways to do this is through the use of affirmations. You can connect with her at:

www.facebook.com/callybocreations
facebook.com/groups/561840101066095
www.instagram.com/callybocreations

Fertility and Loss... My Journey

Amanda Davies

2004. The year I got married. It was the start of my married and family life. We wanted a load of children and, after a couple of years, we moved into our family home. A four-bedroom house we were going to fill.

It was becoming increasingly obvious that nature was not taking its usual course. We sought advice from the GP, who ordered the usual tests. The first of which was to see if I was ovulating. Tests confirmed I was, so I was given some medication to ensure this was happening every month.

After starting this medication, I was very positive that it would just be a matter of time. I always prided myself on the fact that I was pretty fit and healthy, my body worked as it should. Time went by and still nothing. We went back to the GP, who referred us for I.U.I. (intrauterine insemination).

At this point, my husband had tests done. Sperm count absolutely fine, but the motility of the little swimmers needed help. The solution: more breaks from his desk to keep them cool, and a few mineral supplements. Job done!!

I can't even remember the number of times that our cycle got cancelled. The reason being that the stimulating hormones that I had to inject stimulated my ovaries too much. Too much stimulation meant too many follicles being produced and too many follicles meant the chances of us having twins, triplets or even quads was increased and ultimately that meant more risk to both me and the babies.

I had more than two follicles every time we tried.

We decided enough was enough and we were referred for IVF. That 'magical solution' that I never thought in a million years I would need. But in the IVF clinic I ended up.

I will never forget that first time I walked into the clinic... silence! No one in the waiting room looked up and there was almost an over politeness from the staff. I actually could have burst into tears at that very moment. I was 'one of those'; you know, the ones who can't have children and had to have help. Yep, that is exactly the thought that was going through my head.

However, it won't take long, I thought to myself. They do it all for you, so pretty much a done deal, again so I thought. How very wrong I was.

More tests were done to try and determine what the issue was. My husband was fine, so it had to be me then? I am not one that believes things – especially anything scientific or medical – are unexplained. My brain works on the theory that there is a reason for everything.

I was admitted for a lap and dye, a common procedure to determine whether my fallopian tubes were blocked. This was the start to the roller coaster of emotions I would experience throughout our IVF journey. You see I was petrified of having this procedure as it involved general anaesthetic. I am allergic to muscle relaxants that are given when you are given a general anaesthetic. This, looking back now, was the first major experience of anxiety.

The results were that my tubes were clear, but I had a slight case of endometriosis, not enough to cause any problem, and a fibroid, again nothing that would cause me to be unable to conceive. Great! Back on track and IVF would help us have a baby. I would be pregnant soon enough, right? No!

I will never forget the first time I had to inject my medication. I had always considered myself a strong person, physically and mentally, but what I was about to embark on would test this.

I was actually away in London with work when I had to do my first ever injection. Miles away from home and my family and friends and I was about to inject hormones into my body… I had never felt more alone.

I psyched myself up, I had to do it, and indeed I did it. Then burst into tears. I had no idea why, just relief, I guess. I had no idea how it would feel, to actually push a needle into my body. In the grand scheme of things it wasn't so bad.

Thus began our first IVF cycle.

I had a mix of feelings when the eggs were retrieved and fertilised. Nervous, I guess, hoping with everything that it would work. These feelings were ramped up when it came time to pee on those lovely sticks that would become my friends.

I was due in work that day and had planned in my head how I would tell one of my best friends, Lisa, that I was pregnant. Sadly, that was never to come to fruition because the test was negative. The feelings that followed hit me like a ton of bricks, for which I was totally unprepared.

I burst into tears. I felt let down. The hard work had been done for us, the egg was fertilised successfully. So why did my body reject it? Why didn't it do what it was supposed to do? What was wrong with my body? The many things swirling round in my head, along with trying to keep strong and put on a brave face. Something I would later become an expert at.

I got to work to where Lisa was waiting with a comforting hug. Yes, I had a comforting hug from my husband, but felt I had to hold it together for him, because I knew he would be really disappointed too.

A few rounds of IVF went by, still with no luck. The cycles were getting more difficult, again mentally as well as physically.

Then one particular round we had, appeared to be,

as I thought, really positive. The drug I was using to stimulate my ovaries into producing lots of follicles seemed to work really well.

In IVF, the more follicles you produce, the higher the potential for a high number of eggs. You see, not all follicles contain eggs. This cycle I ended up with twenty follicles.

Once the eggs are retrieved, providing you feel okay, you can go home. This time something felt different. You are usually slightly uncomfortable afterwards, but a couple of painkillers and you are okay. Not this time. I felt in pain and ended up going to bed when we got home, which was really not like me. I got up to go to the toilet and nearly passed out. Something wasn't right, I knew my body, I knew something was wrong. In the middle of the night I was sick. It was becoming increasingly apparent a lot of my symptoms were that of hyperstimulation syndrome.

As soon as the clinic opened, I called them. 'Ring 999' was the nurse's response. I was taken to the local A&E, where they did loads of tests to ensure all was okay. I was transferred to the hospital the clinic was based in, so they could keep an eye on me in the gynae ward. After a number of ultrasounds, it looked like I had a mild case of hyperstimulation. Basically, I had produced too many follicles in response to the hormones I was injecting, the risk being that fluid from the egg sacs would leak into my abdomen and into the spaces around my heart and lungs. Most of the time symptoms are mild but for 2-8% of sufferers medical intervention is needed. I was lucky, it was caught early and not serious.

The cycle had to be abandoned and my embryos frozen. That was the lowest I had felt up to that point.

You then have to wait for your body to go through its cycle before you try again. Time being wasted, but nothing I could do. Patience is not my strong point.

After more rounds it still wasn't working. I had implantation failure, and each time it was getting harder.

I was finally tested to check my T cell count. These levels were too high to conceive. My body's immune system was killing the embryos, perceiving them as foreign bodies and, therefore, a threat. I was gutted. This meant I would never become a mum!

We were referred to a professor in Warwick, who was conducting research into the use of steroids and implantation failure. I was prescribed steroids to try alongside my IVF drugs to see if we could trick my body into accepting the embryo. I had hope!

Sadly, this still didn't work.

I was trying to remain positive and strong, but this was slowly fading. In the meantime, friends were getting pregnant. This is the hardest thing ever. You are trying to be happy for them, but inside you are breaking slowly. You go through a whole heap of emotions; happy (for them), sad, angry, jealous... yes, jealous. Then the whole 'it's not fair', 'why them and not me', 'why me'...

This went on for nine rounds of IVF. After the ninth failed, we didn't know what to do next. I was advised to have one more round, and if that didn't work, call it a day. I broke down. That was it, we were not going to become parents. Then anger and stubbornness took over. Give up was not an option.

My background is in biology and clinical research, so I started looking for research into implantation failure. I came across immune therapy and information on a clinic in London who specialised in this. My hopes picked up again.

We discussed it and decided that this was it. We were going to do everything on this round, and it would be our last go.

I spoke to the consultant and he seemed very positive he could help. Here we go! Further tests in London, which confirmed that my immune system was too high, and a plan put in place. I had a renewed sense of hope and positivity.

Treatment started. I had to have a whole array of treatments and drugs, and frequent trips to London for some pretty awful treatments and infusions. My mum came back and forth with me, which was of huge comfort and support.

The actual stimulation started and between my clinic at home and the one in London, a number of eggs were harvested and fertilised. Four made it. We also decided to have our embryos genetically tested to ensure they were all okay.

The day came to have the embryos put back. We travelled to the clinic, nervous to see how many they would be putting back. This is it, we were on the brink of a successful round... nothing is ever straight forward for us. Out of four embryos tested, one had died during the testing, two were abnormal and the last one they couldn't get a reading on. Our options were to retest, but run the risk of it too dying, or put it back and hope for the best. After all that I had just gone through I had to try, or it would have all been for nothing. The embryo was put back and we just had to wait and see. I went home deflated. That's it, it's over!

A day before my pregnancy test, I started bleeding, not uncommon in IVF. I went to the clinic to change medication. Whilst there I did a test, being warned that it may be too early to have a result. Into her office, no expression on her face, I felt sick. That's it, all over.

'Congratulations, you are pregnant!' I couldn't be. Everything had been against us. After everything, I was finally pregnant. I am not one for believing in miracles, but that little embryo was a miracle. That little miracle turned into my beautiful baby girl.

A couple of years later we had another round of IVF. To our astonishment I was pregnant. We went for all the initial scans; it was viable and developing well. We were so happy and thankful.

I was eleven weeks and two days and we were excited for my twelve-week scan. Eleven weeks two days was a Saturday and my world was about to be turned upside down. I started bleeding. I knew something was wrong and we went to the hospital. The consultant confirmed and we heard those dreaded words, 'I am sorry there is no heartbeat.' My heart broke. But I had to put on that brave face yet again, as I had a two-year-old at home.

A number of weeks passed, and my body still hadn't passed my baby. It was getting increasingly hard for me, so I went to hospital to get the process started. I came home that evening and my baby was born. 6th May, 11:45pm. It was so tiny in the palm of my hand. I sat there physically shaking. I wrapped it in a piece of my late grandmother's scarf and placed it in a cardboard box. I was firm in my wishes that it be buried in our garden. The following day it was buried in a pot with a plant that blossoms every year around the time it was born.

As if all this wasn't enough, a week later, my mind and body would be tested again! I started to haemorrhage in the early hours of the morning. We rang 999 and an ambulance took me straight to hospital. As I lay in the ambulance I heard sirens, thinking it was another ambulance passing, then realising it was mine. Straight into resus and the major haemorrhage protocol was initiated. I was haemorrhaging quite badly, and they couldn't stop it. I needed stabilisation to be transferred to another hospital, but they were struggling to do so.

I just lay there and closed my eyes and thought

enough is enough; it's time to just slip away. Then the fighter in me said 'fight God damn it, you have a little girl at home that needs you!!'

I stabilised enough for them to transfer me. The staff acted very quickly and pulled out my placenta, which I hadn't passed, and it was that causing the haemorrhage. The next day I had a D&C to ensure all the pregnancy had gone.

It was time to start healing and enjoy life with my little family.

A few months later, things started to take a downward turn, and I started suffering panic attacks at the thought of losing my family.

That is when a wonderful grief midwife came into my life. Christi-Ann saved me! I owe her so much. She worked through my grief with me and it became evident that I was suffering with hypervigilance and PTSD. I had two rounds of PTSD therapy, which really helped.

Things started to get back to normal, until summer 2019. I started suffering once again and my PTSD symptoms manifested again. It all came to a head on the August bank holiday, in what I can only describe as a breakdown. I eventually went to the GP. They started me on medication to help me through.

I am still on the medication but, using all the tools I have learnt, I am now managing the symptoms and flare ups. If an attack happens, I am able to deal with it and resolve it much quicker. I still have a long way to go, and if it wasn't for the love and support of my amazing husband, Simon, family and friends, I am not sure I would have got through this journey and be where I am today. And to my beautiful baby girl Annabelle, who is my absolute world.

Now it's time to live life and enjoy making memories with my miracle family.

***

Amanda is a forty-something full-time mother to Annabelle. She lives in South Wales with husband, Simon, Annabelle and their family dog.

Her passion is to help anyone going through fertility, and she started a blog focusing on this. The hope is that it will help others that are about to go through or are going through the IVF process, along with trying to help rid the stigma that is still attached to fertility treatment even now.

You can find her blog at:

http://www.theinfertilitybubble.wordpress.com

Or on Facebook at The infertility bubble

How My Divorce Helped Change My Life for the Better

Andrea Binks

I trained to be a dancer and during my final year of dance college I was chosen to perform in the pantomime 'Sleeping Beauty' at the Woodville Halls Theatre in Gravesend. Little did I know that I would meet my future husband in this show. I was a dancer, and he was playing French Frank – the jester and all-round funny guy of the show. I knew almost immediately that I liked him, and I loved how he really was the star of the show. Fast forward eleven years and there we were getting married in 2006 with our first child born just over a year later and our second coming along just over a year after that. I thought I had everything figured out. I was married to my best friend and had two beautiful sons who were kind, loving, funny and intelligent. I had a great job that I loved – life was spot on. How wrong could I be but how right could it all turn out in the end?

I had been working as a presenter on a shopping

channel for many years. I brought in a great income for our family and I managed to balance the pressure of combining a successful career without losing out on precious time with my boys. I was proud of how I had it all worked out. Then along came 2014 and everything changed. It was in 2014 that I learnt of my husband's affair, the shopping channel I had been working for was going to close down, my dog Tia had to be rehomed due to aggressive behaviour and my beloved mum found out she had breast cancer. This was on top of losing my dearly desired third child through miscarriage just the year before. All I could think was 'What had I done to deserve such awfulness?'

It was a Thursday morning, and I was busily cleaning my house to welcome my husband home after his week working away when my phone pinged with a text. A text that I will never forget. Suddenly everything I thought about my life was turned upside down. My husband loved another woman!! WHAT!!! WHO?? HOW!! Of course, he denied it – made up a whole heap of lies surrounding the text but I couldn't bear it. I begged him to tell me the truth. Still to this day I will never know the exact truth, although none of that really matters anymore. We spent that night going round and round in circles and I told him that I would file for divorce in the morning, which he begged me not to do. I remember trying to get away from him all night and I ended up in the spare room. He, of course, followed me and, in the morning, both our boys came running into the bedroom shouting, 'Yesssss, Daddy's home, Team McClean are back together again!' and 'Family McClean on the family raft!' a song that we had all sung together whilst on holiday at Disney World, Florida the year before. They literally threw their arms around us both and were so happy. I looked at my ex and he had tears in his eyes, and I remember him saying, 'I can't break this family up.' Those words will haunt me forever. It was like my feelings didn't even come into it, I didn't matter, and it was his decision what was going to happen next.

As we had our annual family holiday to Spain booked, we still went, and I remember just immense sadness every day. My ex-husband told me that he really didn't want a divorce and asked if we could try again. I agreed for the sake of our children but soon found out that he wasn't going to change. We did try to save our marriage through counselling, but things had changed, and we eventually agreed that it wasn't going to work. This, of course, is the very condensed version of the pain and torture I experienced from not just his words and actions towards me but those of my own mind, and here is where my story starts and what I want to focus on.

During this time, my own mind was such an enemy to me. Negative thoughts filled my head almost every minute of every day. What was wrong with me? Was I not pretty enough? No one else will want to be with me. I am such an awful person to live with.

It was constant. I remember crying myself to sleep, waking up thinking it was all a dream then realising it was actually my reality and crying all over again. I felt so unbelievably lost. I had always been such a strong person (I thought), yet everything I thought I knew was gone. Suddenly there was no security, no familiarity and I had no idea who I was or what I wanted. This wasn't helped by the emotional abuse I was being subjected to almost daily. When the person you love screams at you, an inch from your face, 'Look at the state of you, you are spotty and fat, no wonder I had an affair!' it can't help but sink in.

My divorce process eventually took just shy of five years to complete and I endured some of the toughest experiences of my life to date. Following a completely harrowing experience at the hands of my ex-husband's lies, I decided to stop playing and start fighting through the courts for my freedom and stability for my children. It was August 2014 and my children had been to Florida with their dad for two weeks. This was the first time in their short lives that they had spent such a long time without me and I without them. I was desperate to see them. Not only was I refused the correct details of their return to the UK, I had to wait for my seven-year-old son to message me on his iPad upon his return to Essex to know that I could go and collect them. I was so excited, though; I had missed them so much. It was a hot August that year, so all I was wearing were shorts and a vest top with flip flops. I arrived at their dad's home to collect them and he refused to give me their passports. As I had a non-molestation order in place, I was advised by my solicitor to contact the police to ask for their assistance in having the boys' passports released to me. To the day I die I will never know why the father of my children did what he did next, only he knows the true malice of his actions, but after lying to the police and falsely accusing me of pushing him to the ground and cutting his hand (which never happened), I was wrongly arrested and spent eight hours in a prison cell. Why the police that day decided to believe his lie over my truth I will never know, but that event had a profound effect on me that he will never fully understand. I was eventually released that night without charge as there was no evidence to support his lie but the emotional scar that left was deep. I spent many a day crying and even the smallest of things could set my emotions rolling down a hill. I wanted the pain to be over, I wanted to feel happy again, I wanted my life back, but I knew I didn't want what I had previously had – talk about confused. That's when I found counselling.

I had begun to look for a new career, ways to make an additional income to support my boys and I, as now financially it was all just down to me. I felt like I needed to make enough money to cover two parents' incomes instead of just one and that was hard. Through looking for a new start – a change of direction – and more income, I realised that I wanted to help others.

I wanted to be able to help my children navigate their way round a painful family breakup and also help other women and their children going through similar experiences to avoid all the mistakes I had made. If I could help just one person avoid all the pain, then my life would have meaning again. Something I have strived for in my life every day since. Victor Frankl says in his book *A Man's search for meaning* that the meaning of life is to find purpose and to have laughter. Two things I now hold dear to my heart and I encourage everyone to look for also.

Mind made up, I decided to retrain to become a counsellor. I discovered that I needed to complete a BA Hons degree in Integrative Counselling before I could find work in this area and begin helping people. Retrain? As a mature student? Write an essay? I didn't even know where to begin with essay writing. I also discovered that I needed to have my own counselling – this put me off at first as I had a preconceived idea of what counselling was for. Again, how wrong could I be? I had visited counsellors a few times in the past, but they had never amounted to anything. I guess I just wasn't ready to make a change back then. Now things were different.

Through my own studies, personal therapy sessions and self-reflection, I am now a completely different person to who I always thought I was as a wife. I had been with my ex-husband for twenty years and I fully believe I lost myself during that time. Luckily through my horrendous divorce I have rediscovered 'me' and learnt to love 'me' again too, and for that I am truly thankful.

Self-love is so important. I am so glad that self-love is now accepted as the norm rather than being a dirty word. Being able to look after yourself and your needs is just as important as looking after someone else's needs, even your children's, because if you aren't okay then who is going to take care of them? Self-reflection can really help on your journey to self-love too. Simple things like writing a journal can really help you to look at how your mind is behaving and how you can make changes for the better. Writing things down can really relieve stress too. Just putting pen to paper can put a completely different perspective on situations and allow you that thinking time to really know your true emotions. Too often during my divorce I would rush in with my responses and when your emotions are fragile this really isn't wise. Now I try to wait before I reply, so I can be sure my emotions have well and truly settled back down. I also thoroughly recommend talking therapies. I am a talker – I will talk to pretty much anyone and am lucky to have shared my story with many of my friends BUT it's not the same as seeking professional help from a trained therapist. They will offer you a safe place to be able to explore your own emotions without any kind of pre-determined judgement. If you do choose to seek a counsellor then I highly recommend finding one that has completed their training, is a member of a professional body and also one that you connect with, as the therapeutic relationship between you 'the client' and them 'the counsellor' is quite possibly the most important aspect of all.

I believe my purpose in life is to help others, so I have created 'Green Butterfly Therapy' to assist with life troubles. The Green Butterfly is a safe environment where people can come for assistance with an issue they are experiencing within living. Many of us suffer from anxiety, depression and lack of self-worth at different times in our lives and exploring our emotions and our thoughts can help us gain a better understanding of how to deal with these issues that can arise. Under the umbrella of 'Green Butterfly Therapy' I created 'Divorce Daze', which I am truly passionate about because I have lived the experience and can fully appreciate what my clients are going through. This is where I can utilise my unique experiences to help women and families better cope with their divorce. The feelings of overwhelm, loneliness, sadness, confusion and anger that a divorce brings are all too present within me and I can totally relate to women and families who are in that daze. I also thought it would never end. I remember crying myself to sleep wondering if I was doing the right thing or just feeling like I couldn't cope. Especially when children are involved in a divorce. If you have successfully navigated a divorce and your children weren't dragged into it at all then I salute you because my children did not escape the emotional pain that divorce brings with it. The pain of not seeing your children every weekend and the frustration when your children are let down or used as pawns in the other parent's game of manipulation. It is one of the hardest things I have ever experienced in my life. BUT I am here to tell you that you WILL get through it and that all the emotions will die down and that one day you will suddenly realise that you haven't had to manage the other parent's behaviour or even had to communicate with them in... well, you won't even know how long it's been and it's a lovely feeling.

I do advocate trying to be as amicable as possible with your ex whilst going through your divorce but sadly that is one of the hardest parts of all. No matter how good your intentions are there will always be two sides and two opinions, and two different people's wants and needs. Then the minute money is mentioned, or the childcare arrangements are discussed, it's like showing a red rag to a bull. That said I truly believe being as amicable as possible is by far the most beneficial thing you can do for your children during this difficult time. There was a long time, years in fact, that my ex and I did not communicate. We wouldn't even make eye contact and that was hard for my children. Thankfully, now my ex and I are able to talk and communicate with each other amicably and the difference in my children is visibly noticeable. They seem happier in themselves and almost like a weight has been lifted, so

I do encourage you to find self-love, so you are better able to cope during these difficult times. For self-love and self-worth is what is needed today and always for a brighter future following divorce. If you are on the journey of divorce or separation, then please do reach out and connect.

Much love,
    Binksy.

***

Andrea was born and raised in Essex in the UK. At the age of sixteen Andrea joined Performers College and trained as a professional dancer, singer and actress. This led to Andrea working extensively across the globe until she joined Bid TV as a shopping channel presenter in 2003. Andrea worked as the senior presenter for Bid TV, Price Drop TV and Speed Auction and was also part of the management team heading up a team of assistant presenters whilst conducting the screen tests and training for all new on-air talent.

Andrea was married in 2006, has two boys and her story takes us through her acrimonious divorce that spanned five years.

You can follow Andrea on:

https://www.facebook.com/
groups/1078488372490138/

https://www.facebook.com/AndreaBinksBinksy/
www.Instagram.com/andreabinksybinks
website: www.andreabinks.com

The Scars that Don't Define Me

Angela Poole

You may never use your arm again! One of many defining moments! But I'm getting ahead of myself! Hi, I'm Angela Poole and this is my story. It's a simple story, but with a few twists along the way. I never thought I would be sitting in my office in leafy Surrey in the UK, writing my story. This is thousands of miles from where my story began.

I grew up in sunny South Africa. Yes, I had to add *sunny* in there because as soon as you say South Africa, that's what people think. I had a happy upbringing in a close-knit family. I'm being completely honest here, there are no deep dark secrets here! And if you think this is a rags to riches story, it isn't that either.

I did everything that was expected of me. I was petrified of doing anything wrong! Pretty boring, hey? I worked hard and excelled at school, but I didn't take chances or step out of my comfort zone. I was shy and reserved, I know friends question this today, but it's true! That doesn't mean I wasn't comfortable enough to stand up and deliver drama pieces, but it was always about being in control. I used to put a lot of pressure on myself (all my own doing) and would literally get sick in my stomach. Believe me, it was never my parents, it was all me! This still creeps in every now and again today but not nearly as bad. I wasn't popular but I wasn't unpopular, and I had a lovely group of friends.

I faced tough choices when I left school and was unsure what my future looked like. Sports physiotherapy really appealed to me, but it was really limiting for women at that time and I wasn't one to push the boundaries. So, I studied beauty therapy with the aim of focusing on the holistic side in the future. However, in the subsequent years I realised that it wasn't my passion. It's easy to be consumed with regrets but I don't like to look at my life that way. I met my future husband because of this decision, funny how life turns out!

I got married at the age of twenty-three (well almost, just short of two weeks), which I never foresaw in my future. It's all about the timing and I had met the guy I wanted to spend my life with, so that was the next step. We built our new home, well he did! Did I mention his job was in construction? Although I definitely played a part and we put loads of blood, sweat and tears into our brand-new home. We were happy and comfortable, but that's not to say we didn't have struggles, mainly financial ones. Then on the evening of 7th December 1999, my life took an unexpected turn.

I've always been a dog lover, there's hardly a time I haven't had one. For the first couple of years of marriage, we owned two dogs, Monty (a Boerbul, which is a South African breed similar to a Bull Mastiff) and Sammy (a Staffordshire Terrier). They were both what I like to call second-hand dogs. Monty was a large, powerful dog who had been mistreated and abandoned, so "we" (I was very reluctant) adopted him. I was persuaded because I believed he could provide protection for us. Anyone in South Africa will know, this is needed due to the high crime rate. Monty showed aggressive tendencies, but we mistakenly made excuses for him. Sammy had "issues" with other dogs but miraculously got along with Monty. Probably because of the difference in size, she didn't stand a chance! However, we had two happy years with these two dogs. Then around November 1999, we got a Boerbul puppy, Cassie, with the hopes of breeding. I don't know what we were thinking!! But all seemed good until that night! I always fed them separately because of Sammy's tendency to fight over food. So that's what I did, just like every other night. I was in a bit of a rush as I was due to meet a friend for dinner and had no help as my husband was working late. After Cassie finished her dinner inside, I let her outside and she just went straight to Sammy's unfinished food. Every evening this had become the norm and we thought that Sammy had now accepted it. But she had other thoughts that evening. She took one look at Cassie eating her food and went straight into attack mode.

She chased her around our parked car and started viciously attacking her. Monty, who was on the other side of the house, heard the commotion and joined in with the attack. He was never aggressive towards other dogs, but I believe that dogs will often behave this way as it's a pack instinct. The two of them were mauling a ten-week old puppy! It was horrific!! *What was I going to do?* Sammy hated water, so I thought that was the best option. I tipped their water bowl over Sammy, hoping that would stop the fighting. Unfortunately, Monty took offence to me pouring water over them, so he turned on me.

He jumped up onto my right shoulder to get me out of the way. *Monty, get off me!* No response! So, I tried to push him off me with no success. This was a 50kg powerful dog up against me with poor upper body strength. I'm probably being hard on myself; I don't know a lot of people of my size who would have been successful at "fighting" back! Now this part is a bit fuzzy because I'm not sure whether he pushed me to the ground, or I went voluntarily. At this stage, his mouth was around my right bicep. *Help, help, help!!* I only had one close neighbour while the others were further away, so it seemed little use. *Don't panic, don't*

panic, dogs feed off fear! Stay calm, relax, stop screaming!
These were the thoughts going through my mind.
Monty, it's Mom! It's me! I said in a calm, measured
tone. No reaction! He was treating me like a ragdoll
and tugged my arm from side to side. *Help, help, help!!*
This time much louder in the hope people would
help me. Out of the corner of my eye, I saw a small
gathering of people at my fence, which was a couple
of metres from where I was lying on the ground. I
heard them shouting and making abusive remarks
about Monty but none of them were willing to help. I
later learnt that one of them threw a snooker cue and a
bottle of hair spray over the fence. *Was I really supposed
to use them while I had a dog attached to my arm?* Then I
heard voices shouting, "Shoot the dog, just shoot the
dog!" Out of the corner of my eye, I saw a stranger
climb over my fence. I found out later that my hero
was a new neighbour who I had never met before, and
here he was saving my life! Yes, at this stage I really
believed that Monty wasn't going to let me go! This
could be the end! As this man approached me, all I was
thinking was *please, please don't shoot ME!* So, I turned
my head, and I was willing to sacrifice my arm just to
end this.

Now, I've read many stories of how doubt is cast
on the recounting of traumatic events. Well, when
adrenaline is surging through your body, you block
things out. There were three shots, but I only vaguely
remember the first one. He shot Monty once, who

then turned on him and he had to shoot twice more to kill him. I didn't experience any ringing in my ears, but I was still not aware of that sequence of events. At this stage I was pacing around with my arm hanging limply at my side, instructing my lifesaver where to get the keys to open my gate. The adrenaline was driving all my actions. Another neighbour who had just arrived home with his sister, a nurse, insisted on driving me to the hospital. They were worried the ambulance may take too long and the hospital wasn't too far away. That's when the pain set in! That car trip seemed to take forever, doesn't that always happen with the worst things in life? She calmed me and squeezed my hand while I cried silently with pain. *It's so sore, it's so sore, it's so sore.* I was rushed into the A&E department and was lying on a gurney when my husband arrived. Now, what I didn't tell you and something I actually wasn't aware of was that as Monty jumped up on me, he hooked my earring and ripped my ear. Still to this day I don't know what my ear looked like. But apparently it was hanging and barely attached to the side of my face. It was for this reason that the emergency staff suggested a plastic surgeon, which, of course, I agreed to. None of the pain relief worked but an X-ray showed my arm wasn't broken. It's hard to describe pain but to this day I still haven't felt anything like it. When the plastic surgeon arrived, he did a superficial examination of my arm and he didn't seem too concerned. The plan was to stitch up the puncture wounds from where Monty's teeth had sunk into me and disinfect the area. I said goodbye to my husband, and I was wheeled into the operating room.

This next part was told to me after I woke up after surgery, and aspects were withheld until many months later. My surgeon noticed a large protruding bulge in my right bicep and inserted his finger down one of the puncture wounds and made a startling discovery. My bicep had been ripped to shreds and had become detached from its insertion point. I had lost 60% of my bicep – it was irreparable! The remaining muscle was stretched and stitched back to the top of my upper arm. But my husband didn't tell me that there was a chance it wouldn't work, and I may completely lose function of my arm. I was thankful that he didn't divulge everything, as it was a lot to digest. So, while I was vomiting – that's what happens when you eat before emergency surgery – I absorbed all this information. I spent five days in hospital on powerful antibiotics to eradicate any infection and thankfully there was none.

Then started the long road to recovery! I knew that two uncertain months lay ahead with my arm in a sling. I was under strict instructions to not allow my arm to drop as it took this long for the muscle and tendons to heal. I felt absolutely helpless! I couldn't drive, which is hard for someone who has always been independent, and had to adjust to life temporarily as a left-handed person. Without me even asking, my mom volunteered to pick me up daily to get me out of the house while my husband was working. Now, I see myself as a strong person, but if it wasn't for my parents I wouldn't have healed mentally and physically as well as I did. I think my house would have been a lonely place, especially since we also had two dogs around as a constant reminder. So, Monday to Friday, I spent time at my parents' house and my mom did an excellent job of distracting me. I never sought out counselling, but I talked openly about the ordeal from the very beginning. In my head, I was thankful it wasn't one of our future children or someone else who I would have felt responsible for.

I still to this day don't know why I had complete confidence that my arm would heal. It certainly wasn't a given knowing the details, but heal it did. After two months, the sling was removed, and my arm hung at a right angle. My arm wouldn't straighten! It was stuck! So, months of painful physiotherapy followed to stretch the muscle and straighten the arm. Two further surgeries as well as more physiotherapy over the course of a year had amazing results. My arm straightened to a point of looking "semi" normal and I regained full functionality. Many things contributed to this outcome that I'm eternally grateful for. A plastic surgeon who did a brilliant job repairing my arm, my complete adherence to the healing process and my family. My husband and my parents presented a confident, positive attitude, well that's what I saw anyway.

Over the years, my arm straightened even more with constant use and the only lasting effects are the scarring, a very slightly "crooked" arm and some shoulder pain. And you know what? I have brought up two busy sons and became a personal trainer. Yes, my life took another turn when I decided to qualify as a personal trainer in 2006. And I'm still a personal trainer today as well as many other roles. But for many years I still struggled with seeing my arm in pictures – it always seemed to hang strangely! That's all I could see. "But I don't even notice it!" The words my husband said to me. He was actually right because my scars were on the inside of my arm, so were hardly noticeable. The scars tell my story, and I wouldn't have it any other way.

When I look back, I actually think this ordeal was easier to recover from than some of the challenges that lay ahead. Almost two years to the day, my elder son, Ethan was born on the 5th of December 2001. His brother, Kaelem, came into the world on the 24th of January 2005. As a mother cradling your babies in your arms, you really have no concept of what the future holds. I certainly didn't have a clue. Nothing really prepares you. You can read every book and still there are no guarantees. In almost every aspect of life, there is a manual and you are required to pass a test to be competent in that task. No such thing exists for motherhood. It's scary, unpredictable and you constantly question your decisions and worthiness. At the age of five, Kaelem was diagnosed with ADHD, ASD and learning problems, but I could have told you at the age of two that there were problems. A mother just knows! His childhood was hard. He was hard work. I wouldn't change him for the world, but it has been a roller coaster. He was socially inept, and kids' parties were so awkward. Then there's the judgement. He was judged and I was judged. Sometimes I just wanted to hide under a rock and pretend this wasn't real. Then came our big move to the UK in 2011.

It was a move I wasn't happy about but, in my head, I knew it was the right decision for the future. Moving to the other side of the world away from friends and family was one of the hardest things I've ever done. And those first two years in the UK were tough. I endured Kaelem's periods out of school while we found the right placements as well as applying for his EHCP (Educational Health Care Plan). I avoided any social activities and playgrounds were just a no-go! It was just too stressful; I was constantly on tenterhooks! I have never felt so alone and isolated! Other families looked perfect, why couldn't I have their lives? Why did life have to be so hard?

A major shift occurred over the subsequent years, mainly the self-acceptance of my life, as well as my new home. This journey has been full of highs and lows – the highs really high and lows really low! At times I have felt like I'm in an abusive relationship, but one I can't walk away from – this is my child! I never considered myself an emotional person but wow my emotions have reached new heights. It feels like a wrench is around my heart squeezing it tight and leaving me breathless! That's what it feels like during times of joy and despair. Yes, surprisingly there have been times of joy. I'm proud of what Kaelem's achieved, not in spite of but because of the obstacles he has faced. Of course, now at the age of sixteen we are dealing with the typical teenager behaviour combined with ADHD. But I am much more confident about the future, something I could never have said years ago.

So, who am I today? I am someone who looks at life through different eyes. I am a less judgemental person and I hate the idea of people being put into boxes. Step out of that box and step out of that comfort zone and do things YOUR way. That's what I stand for now. I celebrate my individuality and now stand as a more confident woman. Far from that people pleaser of my childhood and adolescence. It's taken a while, but I've learnt to not forget myself on the shelf and to love my real inner self. And yes, that includes all the flaws and imperfections. I'm still a work in progress, and still learning every day. I am so grateful to my husband who backs and supports me in everything I do. Having a cheerleader like this is invaluable. And, of course, I appreciate all the women I have met and the relationships that I am nurturing in my new women's community. I don't think I'm anyone special, but I hope to inspire women through my story. It's not what happens to you but how you deal with it that counts. I feel like this is *my* time and I'm ready to fly. I know that I wouldn't be in this position if it weren't for the scarring challenges that I have been through. My mental and physical scars tell a story and that's *ME*.

***

Angela, is a forty-six-year-old mum of two teenage boys (sixteen and nineteen) living in Surrey, UK, but originally from South Africa. Her sixteen-year-old has ADHD and ASD and this journey has been a roller coaster. She has learnt many lessons from the many challenges she has faced over the years, which led her to qualifying as a personal trainer and now a motivator and speaker. She is passionate about uplifting and motivating people with her daily raps on Instagram, while always keeping it real and honest.

In the past year she has started a women's community, The Original Woman, supporting women in their journey to becoming more confident and stepping out of their comfort zones. She enjoys making real connections with people and believes her story is inspiring to those wanting to make a real difference in their lives.

https://www.facebook.com/groups/
theoriginalwoman
https://www.facebook.com/theoriginalwomen

For Thinner and for Worse

Carola Kolbeck

'Where feminism taught women to put a higher
value on themselves, hunger teaches us how to
erode our self-esteem.'

Naomi Wolf, 1991, The Beauty Myth

I flick through the tabloid magazines our neighbour
has left for me, drinking in the luxurious dresses, the
extravagant houses, the celeb gossip and hints and tips
for the latest foolproof diet, that one exercise routine
that will help you stay lean and defined, youthful and
attractive. I yearn for a hint of cheekbone and check the
mirror where my boring, pale face and full cheeks stare
back at me. Back with my magazines, I get hooked on a
story about Princess Victoria of Sweden. Once a slightly
fuller-figured teenager, she has now lost weight, and the
magazine is chronicling her demise into full on anorexia
with glee. 'Look at how plump she was. Look how good
she looked when she lost that weight. Look at her now,
just skin and bones.' The world staring, the media writing
their narrative, readers judging and pitying the ghost of a

girl who stopped eating. I compare those before and after pictures. My eyes hover over the protruding collarbones and clavicle. I feel my own. They stick out, but not enough. I want to look like her. I want to be as thin as her. I think she looks much better now. Skinny is good. Skinny is beautiful. Skinny is my new dream.

I was never a skinny child, but I wasn't podgy either. I was a healthy weight with chubby cheeks and a curved spine that made my bum stick out. However, my earliest childhood memories about my body are looking at my friends, wishing I was like them: skinny and small with blonde, straight hair. I hated that I was the tallest in my school year. In class photos I was towering over everyone, even the boy I fancied. But even with my dodgy haircut, courtesy of my mum, hand-me-down clothes and no sense of style, I was a popular girl and a straight-A student. My insecurities were my own, but never justified by others. That was, until a PE lesson when I was nine years old. We were practising handstands, when my PE teacher, a scrawny, balding man in his late fifties, chuckled.

"You should lay off the potatoes!" His comment left me stunned. I was unable to say anything, feeling dumbstruck and shocked. I remember going home in floods of tears and my mother, outraged, called the teacher. I never got an apology, and somehow those comments stuck. Clearly, I must be unshapely, dumpy and clumpy, if even a teacher said so.

A few years later, standing in the lift on the way up to my weekly ballet class, one of my dancer friends poked me and grinned: "You've got some puppy fat on you!" Speechless, I let the words pierce my skin and form a knot in my throat. Ironically, a few months later, that same girl pointed out how skinny I was. Nature had done its thing and made me grow, made me develop, as puberty hit, and as I left my childhood body behind and grew into my teenage one, I wished someone had told me that I had nothing to worry about back then, now, or in the future. That my body was going to do its thing and as long as I kept on eating healthily, exercising regularly, and cherished that amazing thing that kept me alive, then all would be fine.

But no one did. So, I stayed in this tall, gangly and awkward body for a few more years, battling with bad skin and the usual teenage stuff of falling in and out of crushes on boys that had no interest in me, until, one autumn, I was so heartbroken that I couldn't eat one evening. The next morning, when I woke up, my stomach was as flat as a pancake. 'Interesting,' I thought. And so, I ate a little bit less every day. By the time it was my fifteenth birthday, I only weighed 50kg. A few weeks later, my mother declared me anorexic and a bitter and emotion-fuelled battle erupted that would last until I left home, four years later. What had begun as my own weight loss experiment to fit into a size six, became my illness that gripped its bony, vicious claws into me and tricked me into thinking I was being hugged tight. I was being dragged to the family doctor who told me to "just eat", which I said I would, with a sincere smile. Of course, I didn't. Late spring, less than six months after my fifteenth birthday, I was admitted to the same hospital I was born in, weighing less than 35kg, and told I was going to die. Unless I ate. I was given two days to stabilise my weight by eating normally. If unsuccessful, I would be fed through a tube as a last attempt to save me.

I'll never forget those two months in hospital, locked up and shut away from the outside world. I shared my room with various girls, all of whom left before I did. One of them, half my age, pointed out she'd never seen anyone with such skinny wrists before. Another one also had an eating disorder. We talked about how much we hated our "fat" bodies, we asked each other about dieting tricks, talked about calorie counting and drinking litres of water before a weigh-in. We chuckled when we planned how we would start dieting again as soon as we were out of hospital. And so, after two months, as I reached my goal weight, a mere 50kg, I was discharged and sent home, and stopped eating that same day. I also cancelled therapy not long after, since my therapist had, in conversation, told me I looked like an ironing board with peas, referring to my non-existent breasts. As the weight dropped again, so did my mood, and by my next birthday I was so low in both weight and spirit that, one night lying in bed, I listened to my heartbeat get slower and slower.

'This is it, I am dying,' I thought, and let go. I didn't die. But I weighed myself the next morning. 33kg. I looked in the mirror. And there, for the first time, I saw me. The real me. Emaciated, the skin stretched over every single one of my exposed bones. Lifting my shirt, I counted the ribs and stared at my bruised hip bones. There was hair everywhere, little, fluffy hairs all over my body and my face. My body was fighting so desperately to keep me alive and warm, when all I was doing was killing it off. And so, I started eating. And after gaining some much-needed weight, I booked myself into a rehab facility far away from home. It wasn't a great stay. I learnt I wanted to live and that I wanted to be free, but I also found I was angry. Very angry. When I got home, I carried on eating. And throwing up. I kept gaining weight and my face became swollen from all the purging and puking. I cut off my hair only to realise that I hated it and found myself even uglier than before. I was in a new hell, and one I couldn't control anymore. I started hitting myself, first with my fists, then with items, in blind rages, until my thighs and legs were black and blue. One night, after a particularly nasty argument with my mother, I climbed out of my window on the top floor, dangled out my legs and looked down. Whatever stopped me from jumping, I don't know. I just knew I wasn't ready to give up and die. And so, I carried on living in my misery, in that new body I kept abusing – now also with cigarettes – and spent more time with friends, let school slip and stopped revising for my final exams. When I finally left home to move abroad, my mother thought she was sending me to my death.

When people ask me what saved me, I certainly have to credit my adoptive home, but, as I recently acknowledged, I actually saved myself. I was always psychologically savvy to know that I was ill, and that only by working hard and having lots of setbacks along the way, could I one day overcome the illness. My head might never fully recover, but it could learn to prevent any future episodes. I was also under no illusions that my self-destructive behaviour could have long-term effects on my health. Aged nineteen, I had never had a natural period and I was well aware of the dangers of brittle bones later in life. Far from home and totally responsible for myself, I got stuck into therapy once more. My therapist was competent and to understand why I had stopped eating, guided me back to my childhood. I had been loved, had great and secure friendships and was an overachiever and perfectionist at school. However, I realised that the early childhood traumas of family deaths had left their mark. I spent my life telling myself and others I had been fine, when I had never grieved properly. I also recognised that I was strong and resilient and brave. That I was sitting there, in a foreign country, financially independent, educated and responsible enough to take action, all by myself, and wanted to live, wanted to be healthy, in mind and body.

And so, I carried on, day after day, year after year. I had my setbacks. I still ate and sometimes purged. I still thought I could be slimmer. I also got told that I may not have children. I cursed myself for my stupidity and drank too much too often. I got into a relationship with a man much older than me and let him take advantage of me, lie to me and wasted over a year of my life, my hopes and dreams on him. My search for approval, for love and peace made every relationship end in total disaster. If I was loved, I ran away and searched for something new, and if I was treated badly, I clung on, desperate to make something work that was beyond broken. And then I realised that I was never going to find it in others. I was only ever going to find it within me. I had to find approval, love and peace for myself within myself. No one could ever give that to me.

One day, not long after that revelation, I found myself surprised at the fact that, not only had I stopped throwing up, but I had also learnt to feel full again and to stop eating at the right time. I was able to enjoy treats without feeling guilty and, instead of seeing hunger as a triumph, I got "hangry" and welcomed food to fuel myself again.

Fast forward seven years, and I have two healthy children and a healthy, strong body. Turns out, when I started taking care of my body, it took care of me again. After years of avoiding certain foods, I allowed myself to spread butter on toast and have chips – both of which I hadn't eaten for nearly fifteen years. Now I rarely think about what I should and shouldn't eat and let my body decide what feels right. I am surprised to learn that, most of the time, I can trust my gut and it'll make the right and nutritious choice for me. Who knew? My mind is also slowly catching up. Having children has certainly changed my perspective of myself, how I talk to myself and what I want from my body and life in general. I want my kids to appreciate their bodies and understand we are all different and that beauty cannot be prescribed by the media, society or what other people think. I want them to have healthy eating habits, and therefore I have to act as a role model. In addition, negative comments about parts of my body I am not keen on are banned for life, even if they may enter my mind.

The skin on my belly will always fold a bit because I carried two big babies to term, the boobs are so small from breastfeeding that I struggle finding a bra. Those faint white stretch marks on my bum are an eternal reminder that I had to gain weight fast to survive. My long, muscly legs carried me my whole life and ran two marathons. My thin arms will always make me look a bit like a monkey but are still strong enough to carry my kids and give some damn good hugs. I never liked my face and found it too chubby, too fat, too this, too that: it's finally a face I like, I appreciate and cherish, and I don't delete photos anymore. It carries two healthy eyes, a sensitive nose and a mouth that, so I am told, has the best smile ever. And then my mind, my fragile, strong, weird, sensible, crazy, constantly-working-overtime mind: it has the power to get me things I really want and is home to feelings of empathy, humility and kindness. Nevertheless, I will probably always have to work hard to keep my mental health in the positive, and I am currently battling with severe anxiety that rules a lot of my life. People say you shouldn't have any regrets, and maybe one day I will be able to believe that too. But, at present, I do have regrets. I wish I'd never starved myself and let myself become so ill. I see the lost time, the opportunities and fun I missed out on because I was either locked up in hospital or rehab or feeling either too fat or thin to go wherever my friends went. I also wonder whether my body would be different today had I allowed it to mature naturally, rather than stump its growth in the middle of puberty.

If I had the chance to talk to my younger self, I would embrace her and hold her so tight, sit and cry with her, as I am crying now whilst writing this. I would tell her that she is so loved, cherished and valuable beyond measure. I would assure her that no thoughtless comment uttered from adults or peers could ever ring true in the light of her natural beauty. I would promise her that she can trust her body and her mind to do the right thing, and just let go, enjoy herself and her life, which is passing by in an instant. Trust the process, trust your mind, body and soul and be you. You are unique, beautiful and valuable.

***

Carola is a writer, published short story author and teacher and is passionate about kindness, integrity and love. She loves leopard print and finally enjoys having her picture taken. You can find her on Instagram, Facebook and Twitter as @chameleoninhighheels.

The Years That Taught Me the Most

Charlotte Cloke

When I started thinking about when my complicated relationship with my body started, it wasn't when I was a child or as a hormonal teen; whilst I had my fair share of uninvited pimples and stretchmarks as a teen, I don't remember ever worrying that I was fat! My parents enforced in me that I was beautiful, and I felt it.

I don't think I really started worrying about how my body looked until I was about nineteen years old.

I remember one of the first times I truly felt ugly, I was stood in my boyfriend at the time's hallway doing my hair in the mirror and his mother came down the stairs. She exclaimed at how different I looked, and I told her I had put some makeup on. 'Oh, charlotte,' she said, 'you must wear makeup, you look so much better.'

I remember going home and sobbing that night, and I think that really was the start to where I am now.

My relationship with my body grew worse over the next four years. I'd go on to have a son a year later, at just twenty years old. I was nervous that people were judging me; I was young, after all. I had very little support from my boyfriend at the time and he would often tell me to lose weight along with several other daily insults. Whilst others longed for chocolate and flowers, I longed for just one kind word from him.

We had a lot going on back then, my son and me. My son's dad tried to kill himself, then decided he didn't want to be a dad or partner, then when he came to collect his things got arrested for hurting me whilst my son was in my arms.

I had to prove back then I was a good mum. I made the mistake of putting my son's dad before him, and whilst I proved I'd never do it again, I live with the knowledge and regret that I did that back then, further reinforcing my useless feeling. I'd quite often put my ex first, before me and my son, in front of anyone. It's hard for me to admit to this, but I did. I felt some sort of responsibility for his mental health, as if somehow it was my fault if he hurt himself.

He convinced me my parents were toxic and I needed to cut them out of my life, and so my friends followed one by one. After years of on and off again, and him not wanting to be a dad or a partner, I found out I was pregnant with my little girl. I knew this couldn't go on, I knew things had to change, but I was in a loop. I gave him one last chance to change, as he said so many times before that he would, and then he hurt my son and me.

That was it.

I was done.

Years of physical, sexual and emotional abuse and my relationship with my body and mind had crumbled. I became a shell of the bubbly and confident woman I was before. At twenty-three, after telling him to leave and having the courage to keep it that way, I sought help. The Susie Project and counselling that I had to save up for was the only way I was going to get through this. I was having to learn to love my body all over again. I had some wonderful friends that got me through this time, ones that I'll be forever grateful for. I'm so glad that despite my worrying distancing from my parents, they stuck by me through thick and thin.

So, my journey to love myself, body and mind started at twenty-three years old. I started learning about myself again, what I liked, and how to express my sexuality freely again. It's hard to do, after all that you feel like you don't deserve anything.

The Susie Project works with men and women who have experienced domestic abuse and who have left their partner. They help rebuild self-esteem and confidence via outreach and then support groups. They also have a 'toolkit' for learning about healthy relationships again as once you've been in an abusive relationship, it's incredibly hard not to fall into that pattern again.

So once I had started this toolkit with The Susie Project, I started learning that the behaviours I'd had for the last four years were not normal or acceptable. I started talking to other women who had been through what I had been through and realising together that my ex was a type of man who would never change and was following a pattern of dangerous behaviour that would only get worse.

Counselling allowed me to talk about what I was going through. I was diagnosed with PTSD and I had EMDR therapy to treat it. EMDR therapy is eye movement desensitisation and reprocessing. It's a form of psychotherapy. You're asked to recall the distressing images, memories or things you've been through whilst the therapist directs you to bilateral stimulation, which is like side-to-side eye movements or hand movements. It's based on a study that negative thoughts, feelings and behaviours are the result of unprocessed memories. The treatment means that when you think of these things in the future, you're able to deal and process them better. It worked for me massively and it stopped me from being a jabbering wreck having severe flashbacks all the time, to being happy, and able to cope with these things.

I really focused on getting me sorted so I would never ever go back to him and could be the best mum for me and my babies, and two years on I think I've succeeded, despite his attempts.

I got play therapy for my son too and oh my

goodness the change that allowed in him was unbelievable! Over some time he started growing more confident again, less scared of himself and others around him, fewer meltdowns, and less reactivity to sound. Before he was struggling with simple things like going to the shops and people being close to him, men being near him and near me or Edith, children or anyone near his things, and he would barely eat, as if it was the only thing he could control.

By twenty-four I felt confident again, still anxious and not back to myself yet, but ready to come off sertraline, and live life again. I decided to start dating again. I was ready to spot if a man was good or not, I knew what I wanted and I knew what the kids and I deserved, and so I just went for it.

I downloaded Tinder!

Not the most traditional way to meet the man of your dreams, but what is a lone parent to do? I can't be going out every weekend and at least this way I could screen them in a way as to who I was going to give time to. I met a few men, all lovely, but really not my cup of tea, and some that quite honestly were only after one thing, and that's just not ever been me.

Until I swiped right and came across a man I can only describe as literally my type, shockingly dark hair, amazing bluey-green eyes! Tall, dark, handsome! The dream! I thought, why not! I'll message him!

He messaged back and we got talking. I was very intrigued, he seemed like the loveliest guy, but I was worried. Beyond worried, actually, that he'd not be able to cope with me or the fact I had two kids or any of the baggage that came with me. He seemed far too lovely to ruin with all that, so what did I do? I told him I couldn't meet up with him; after making him wait three months, I decided I couldn't meet up with him.

A month went by and I could not get him off my mind. I was getting on with life, trying not to think about him and trying to keep happy and the kids happy, I was healing and going to my rebuilding groups, still following what I'd been told and keeping the kids' biological dad away from them. I was doing everything to keep them safe, I was being a good mum.

Christmas came around, just before actually, and I had been messing around with the kids and Snapchat filters. We posted them on my story, and I had a message come back from him: "You look beautiful and all so happy." All I could muster to say back was: "I miss you," and that started our conversation again.

Christmas went and family stuff and birthdays and then finally in January I plucked up the courage to agree to a date. By this point I felt I trusted him and knew him enough. I told my best friend so she knew, just in case he was a secret weirdo, and we had our first chilled movie date. I remember thinking he looked way better than in photos and there was no way he would see me again as I was a fat lump!

He said I was beautiful and perfect, and I started to really feel it. He made me feel beautiful and I felt like for once I didn't have to hide my lumps and bumps, I didn't have to worry about my secrets or baggage, not having make up on or anything. He made me feel beautiful with all of that.

After a while, I introduced him to my children and it's safe to say they fell hard and fast for him just like I did. They asked to call him Daddy and he agreed, and my heart grew fuller with love for him every day.

One of the biggest things was the love I was growing for myself again! With him by my side, I could do anything.

By my twenty-fifth birthday, I was a five-times bestselling worldwide author and illustrator.

I knew I was beautiful and there was nothing that was going to ruin that, even on my wobbly days (and I still have a fair few!). My babies were happy, and they had everything they needed and so did I, for once. They're happy, I'm happy, body and mind, and now I can see a future that's exciting in front of us. I know he's the one, cheesy, but I've known that from the moment I set eyes on him. I knew I wanted a family with him and he made it very clear from day one that's what he wanted too. In week two we were already in love, that was clear, by three we knew it was forever and by week four we were looking at houses to buy. I think to most that might sound a little crazy, and honestly whilst I have always believed in true love, I never ever thought I'd find it.

My kids call him Daddy (their choice) and to them

he is their daddy, he's the one that's there day or night, who hugs them when they need hugging and loves them no matter what, like I do. I am truly lucky to have him as my partner and love us the way he does. I certainly couldn't have got through this last year without him!

When we had been together for a while, we started trying for a baby. We had two miscarriages. I was so frustrated, how could I fall pregnant so easily with a man who didn't deserve children and struggle so hard with a man who is an amazing daddy? Then on the third attempt, when we had really started to lose hope that it was an option for us, after time and a lot of praying… we fell pregnant again.

And that baby is still growing inside me as I write this. I am so excited to have his baby; to give this baby a daddy who is kind and selfless and puts his family first is so exciting. I know I'll always be able to rely on him because I already can with my children I have now. This has already been such an amazing experience, the excitement of being pregnant, actually trying for a baby and the love I see that he already has for this baby is so refreshing. Because I already have a love for this baby that's half me and half him.

I never thought I'd have any more children, mostly because I thought I was going to be alone forever. I didn't care for being with anyone again, the thought of it all was too much for me, but I did it and found the love of my life, and I'm a lucky one.

Whilst I have found my happy ending, the battle still goes on. I had reported the abuse that myself and my son sustained and despite having lots of evidence, it wasn't enough for a conviction. All bail conditions keeping us safe were dropped and now all we have is an injunction against my ex.

I've also been battling in family court as my ex got a new girlfriend and decided to take me to court for access, I suspect to prove something to her. Despite the astounding evidence in front of them that I had been advised to keep him away from the kids for their safety, the court ruled that I had alienated him from the children and gave him full unsupervised contact. I and my children have been propelled back into abuse and there's absolutely nothing I'm able to do about it for fear of them being ordered to reside with him, further propelling them – my son especially – into abuse.

No one has considered the effects on my son at all, and even now whilst we await a first date of contact and they're just having video calls, I cannot even explain the effect it has had on him. He becomes a completely different boy within a second. And it's heartbreaking because I'm having to force him into something I really don't want to. I did my job to keep them safe and now that's been completely taken away from me.

I have no answers to what the future will hold for my children. It's all incredibly foggy at the moment, I don't know what will happen, or how they'll cope, I just have to keep taking my son to therapy and hope that it continues to help him despite being back in abuse again. I have to hope he will speak up for his little sister who is unable to speak properly yet, and I have to hope that Neil and I always being a safe and stable home to come back to is enough to keep them from struggling even more and having life-long effects from this.

I have to hope, because without that I would lose my mind worrying about the what ifs. The control isn't mine anymore, and that's hard because it's my job to make sure they're safe. As a mum it's hard to step away from that, and honestly a little soul destroying, but what's harder as a survivor of abuse is handing the control to the man who raped, beat and emotionally, mentally and financially abused you and your child.

I have no answers, but I hope it helps someone else feel not alone, there is nothing worse than that. For now I have to focus as much as I can on the good things in line for us as a family, and there is so much ahead, a baby, a house, spending the rest of my life with Neil.

I have the dream, I have come so far and achieved more than I ever thought I could, it's just ever so slightly in a shadow at the moment... some day the sun will come out again.

***

Charlotte Cloke is a children's book author and illustrator and has written and illustrated a book for children who have been through trauma and abuse. Whilst she is no expert, she is a mum navigating her way through parenthood with a child who has PTSD. Sometimes the only way to talk about things in an age-appropriate way is through the calm of a bedtime story.

Books:

Terrance the Triceratops Troubling Time
www.amazon.co.uk/terrance-triceratops-troubling-charlotte-cloke

Perry's Positivity Planner
https://fuzzyflamingo.co.uk/product/charlotte-cloke-perrys-positve-planner/

Only If You Knew

Charlotte White

Growing up, I always wanted to be a nurse; I loved caring for people. I'm not sure why, but I think it may have been because my mum used to often help look after the elderly in the accommodation opposite us. I remember the adrenaline rush I used to get when my shift ended and I left the building, knowing that I had done my best to help someone that needed it and that I had been there for them in their last few hours on this world.

For as long as I can remember, I have loved supporting and helping others. I remember sweeping the paths free from snow for our elderly neighbours and helping my mum look after my brother.

I have always got such a warm feeling inside when I know I have helped someone. Be it my own family, one of the children, one of their friends or a complete stranger. I suppose that's why I do what I do today. However, if you had said to me when I was little or even about seven years ago that I was going to have a BA (HONS) Degree in Social Care, be raising awareness for cancer, supporting mummies through a blog and be a Wellness Mentor, I would have laughed at you.

My journey started about seven years ago when I took the step to study Health and Social Care at degree level. My children had all come of school age and I was not working, so what better time to better me? This was not an easy decision to take; I kept telling myself I was too old and was not good enough to do a degree. After many sleepless nights and extreme amounts of stress, I graduated with a BA and was so excited to step out of my comfort zone to start my new venture helping to support so many more people.

Finding a job was not as easy or straightforward as I had first thought. My husband was working away at the time and, not living near any family that could help, I had to work around the children. I applied for several jobs, heard from some and some nothing. The one interview I was offered I was unable to attend because of mum duties right at the last minute.

The constant knockbacks and not hearing from applications started to take a toll on me. I was starting to become really fed up and feeling so lonely with the hubby working away. I had never faced so many challenges when looking for a job before. With the hubby working away, when the children had gone to bed I was alone and felt so fed up, so would often have a glass of wine and scroll the internet. Not being able to find work really started to get to me, especially sitting on my own most nights. I was becoming desperate to socialise and talk to other adults. Scrolling the internet I came across mums that shared their challenges in life, so I decided to set up a Facebook page and started sharing my challenges in the hope I may help another mum or even get a job from it and make my brain function again. I shared how my day had gone, if it was productive and if I had heard from a job. If I was feeling low and fed up, I would share that as well.

Summer had arrived, so I decided to give up on the job hunting and enjoy the holidays with the children. Little did I know, though, that my world was about to come crashing down on me and my family thanks to cancer.

In the summer of 2017, my husband was diagnosed with bowel cancer, which came as a huge shock to all of us. He had been poorly for a while, but it would seem he had not been telling me everything, as I was about to find out, which made me feel hurt that he felt he could not talk to me and scared about what else he was keeping from me.

At the beginning of the summer, my husband started to have tests after being referred by the doctor to the hospital. During a colonoscopy they found some polyps, which they took biopsies from; they were being tested for cancer. When I heard those words, I immediately said, 'That's it, you have cancer!' I always think the worst of the situation and, in this case, I could not have been more right. The following few weeks where so hard. I had to put on a brave face for the children and for Roger all the time, whilst having to hold myself together and talking to no one. I was keeping a huge secret and yet Roger was talking to his boss and the medical staff. I hated him for this and yet he had no choice but to talk to these people.

The weeks leading up to the diagnosis were incredibly hard. I felt like I went into overdrive and was living with this huge secret that I could not even talk to Roger about because the atmosphere between us was surreal and tense. I wanted to make Roger better and make it all go away, but I couldn't, which made me feel useless in a way. Why us? Cancer is something old people get, not someone young and active. When the diagnosis finally came, I literally felt like my world had come crashing down on me. I broke down in tears but only for a matter of minutes, it was strange. I had to pull myself together and be strong for Roger and the children; we were going to get through this.

The day after the diagnosis we told the world, well Roger did. I was scared and didn't want to. I suppose by doing this it all felt real, the bubble we had been living in for the past few weeks had been burst. The number of messages and individuals reaching out to Roger mostly was overwhelming. The emotions and reality of it all was becoming so much more real. This I suppose was the real start, when thinking about it, of my emotional roller coaster ride of cancer. Feeling lonely, angry, frustrated, sad, confused, the list goes on and I had no control over these emotions, no matter how hard I tried.

I was not the one with the cancer, my husband was, so it's only right that he gets all the attention, support and care. So why did I almost feel like I was jealous of all the attention he was getting? He was the one that had the cancer. But what about me? I'm the one that had to watch my husband have drugs pumped into him making him become so ill, I'm the one that had to talk to the teacher when the youngest had breakdowns in school, whilst another child is scared Dad won't be around for Christmas. Oh, and to keep all emotion in as I had to be strong for Roger and the children, but I had no one to be strong for me. I felt alone, all I wanted was a hug and to be told everything would be okay. I wanted to be spoken to at appointments and not looked down to. I wanted to be asked if I was okay and for people to stop telling me what to do and how to act in front of Roger and the children.

Things started to get too much for me. I had no family near me and only a few friends that really got it. Spending many nights on my own, I would often open up a bottle of wine and have a glass or two, which soon turned into every night. I would get the children settled and open the bottle and then go and have a cigarette, hiding away from the children. Standing and looking at the stars, hoping my nanny was at least looking over me, tears would fall down my cheeks as I let all the emotion go from the day. Why us? All I want is a hug, all I want is someone to think about me, how I'm feeling and how all this is for me. I would often sleep on the sofa as all I wanted was to be alone, going over and over everything that was going on. I had so much emotion going through my body things often ended up in some sort of heated discussion with Roger. I found it so hard that he got all the support and attention, and I was left to it. Roger was fully aware of how I was feeling, which made me feel worse, as he was the one with cancer and he was comforting me. I felt so wrong for feeling the way I did, but I could not control my emotions, I was scared and so lonely, but at the same time never wanted anyone to help, I just wanted someone to think about how I was feeling.

Supporting someone through cancer is hard, especially when you have a family as well. With all the running around I neglected my needs to the point that I became exhausted during one of Roger's operations, but I continued plodding on. I survived on tea and fags during the day and wine and fags on a night, hiding outside so the kids did not see me. Food was the last thing on my mind, my appetite had more or less gone, resulting in me losing a lot of weight. I felt useless and alone and became so frustrated with everything going on. I wished people would realise that the impact of cancer was on more than just Roger on this journey.

I was struggling with this, but at the time would never admit it, as to me I was doing just fine. I had a blog that was about mummies, so decided to start sharing my journey and what we were going through as a family with cancer in it. The highs, the lows, from telling the children their dad had cancer to the first chemotherapy cycle. The emotion was there still, and the anger and frustration. By sharing what I was going through or us as a family I started to feel relief as I was no longer building up all the emotion inside me. When people started to comment and reach out to me, I started to realise that all I was feeling was normal. Crying in front of the children was fine, the emotions I was feeling were normal and cancer is a journey that has an impact on all the family, not just one, and loneliness is also a normal feeling.

By me sharing my journey of cancer, I came to not only realise that my emotions and all we were going through was normal, but that there was very little support out there and cancer was a topic not spoken about very much. The more people reached out to me and commented on my posts the more it made me determined to carry on sharing what I was going through; if I could help at least one person then my job was done.

The more and more I wrote and the further the journey went on, I started to feel better about me. I was learning so much from blogging and sharing my journey, the highs and the lows, that I started to turn things around. One day I was outside having a fag and wondered why I was smoking! My hubby is coming through treatment for cancer! I don't think I even finished the fag; he went back into hospital at Easter for another operation. I bought a packet of fags, as I felt I needed them. I think I did, but I have not bought a pack since and that's nearly two years ago. I also stopped drinking so much and started to run, something I had never ever done before.

I remember looking at my hubby and seeing this individual that was becoming frustrated; he was going through so much but, to me, he was not as active as he could have been. He had been unable to run due to the cancer. It was strange but I had been thinking about it for a while, and it just came out. I want to start running, will you come with me and help me, as I've signed up for the Race for Life!

Seeing him run made me feel good. I was rubbish and wanted to quit so many times. I cried and put myself down so often but, with the support of Roger, I kept at it and took part in the Race for Life on behalf of my hubby who was in remission for bowel cancer.

My page was growing, and I was starting to help so many people it felt amazing. I was going out for runs on my own and really feeling and seeing the change in me. I had helped Bowel Cancer UK in recording a short clip for International Women's Day and shared our journey in a magazine.

Then life got in the way and it all came to a halt again. It was like this for over a year. I kept saying I was going to start working out and never bothered, the same as my blogs. Then the world almost started shutting down due to the pandemic. School shut and the children started to do home schooling. One lesson was PE with Joe Wicks with the youngest. I remember doing the first session and I felt it so much the day after, I could not sit down without being in pain. It was then that I realised how unfit I had become, and it was time to do something about it. I often got up and did Joe's PE lesson on my own, the youngest was not having any of it. After a few weeks, I was starting to really get the feel for it as I was starting to feel so much better within me. The summer holidays arrived and the PE lessons stopped. I was still working out and was really getting into it. I was starting to feel like me and then one day after having the same conversation with the hubby more than once, I took a huge step and became a Wellness Mentor with Beachbody. It was not an easy decision, but after connecting with my coach and hubby saying go for it, I did and didn't look back. Yes, I was scared at the beginning and still am, I still have a long way to go, but I look in the mirror and see I'm slowly seeing me again.

Yes, my anxiety is still there, I'm still learning to accept my body and love me for me. Every day I become stronger in body and mind. I surround myself with people who love me and look at life in a totally different way. Travelling the journey of cancer and becoming a Wellness Mentor, I'm pushing myself daily and stepping out of my comfort zone to help me and others. I'm doing what I love and cannot wait to continue growing and reaching for my dreams.

***

Charlotte White lives in Wales with her husband and four children. She is a Wellness Mentor, mummy and cancer blogger and someone with a passion to help raise awareness for cancer. You're never too young.

https://www.wondermami.co.uk
https://www.facebook.com/TheWonderMami/
https://www.instagram.com/thewonder_mami/

In Love with the Shape of Me

Claire Ashton

"You are SO fat, it's disgusting."

"You are a FAILURE."

"You look horrific."

"You are such a BAD mother."

"I HATE you."

I stood there in floods of tears. The guilt washed over me and I felt disgusted at myself. I felt I deserved every word.

Except it wasn't someone else saying those things to me. It was me saying them to myself, looking in the mirror on that hot summer's day. I'd given birth to my much-wanted baby a week previously and just stepped off the scales showing a six-stone weight gain. I'd had a love-hate relationship with the scales and my body for a long time and this was the rock bottom point for me.

***

I grew up doing a lot of physical activities as hobbies – gymnastics, swimming, horseriding and three different types of dance. When I gave up these activities in my mid-teens, I gained weight. In my head I was the fat girl amid a sea of skinny friends, although looking back I was about a size fourteen. I lost the weight when I went to university and then my twenties became a decade of yo-yo dieting. I discovered the gym when I was twenty-four and exercise became part of my life again. Whenever I fell off the diet wagon, which happened a LOT, I'd exercise more and everything would be okay again. Be "good" with my diet and exercise well, be "bad" with my diet and exercise even more. In the six months leading up to my wedding, my diet was "clean" (read: I had a very long list of bad foods I avoided and a much shorter list of "good" foods that I ate), my exercise levels were increased, I felt that I had total control and a very strong grip on it all. I walked down that aisle feeling happy with how I looked. I was probably a total nightmare to be around, though, my husband is too nice to say!

We decided to start trying for a family immediately and whilst I managed to get pregnant quickly, I unfortunately suffered a number of miscarriages. My first one happened at twelve weeks – just before the so-called "safe" zone when the risk dramatically drops. I'd almost got there... then, bam! Not this time. When I had my second miscarriage, I felt my world start to crumble. I'd read that one miscarriage was common and thought I'd had mine, so I'd be fine. This threw up a lot of questions for me. Had I done something wrong in my past? What was wrong with me? Why couldn't my body keep a pregnancy?

As well as feeling so incredibly sad, I had guilt that I had failed these babies too and a huge responsibility that my body had done something wrong. Was I not good enough to become a mother?

When I became pregnant with my son, I was warned it was likely I'd miscarry again. Whilst I didn't miscarry, my mind and body were so stressed and I was anxious and scared for the entire pregnancy. I was considered a high-risk pregnancy; I couldn't exercise and the weight piled on. I comfort ate for the whole nine months, craving all those foods that were on my "bad" list. I also developed SPD (also called PGP) – a painful condition during pregnancy which can cause restricted, difficult movement. I needed crutches to walk and wore an attractive girdle belt and support bandage feeling pain with every step.

All the control of the food I'd eaten and the exercise I pushed my body to do disappeared. When I weighed myself a week after giving birth to my son, I was nearly six stone heavier than I had been on my wedding day fourteen months earlier. Six stone in fourteen months – I felt awful and that I was a failure. I was a nurse and a qualified personal trainer, I should have known better. I had done this to me, no one else was to blame.

There is only one photo of me with my son when he was a baby, just one! I simply wanted to hide away as I was so disgusted with myself. I felt that I had let myself go and let myself down.

If this were a fiction book I'd now tell you how I had an epiphany when he was born, lost the weight, never tried to have an iron clad control over my body again and lived happily ever after.

Real life isn't like that, though, as we all know.

What did happen was that I hit rock bottom with my self-esteem and confidence. I knew that for the sake of my son and myself I needed to climb back up. It helped that my son wasn't a great daytime sleeper, so I would walk every day pushing the pram around the wonderful city I lived in. Maternity leave meant time to cook more and I decided to try something new – eating a balanced diet of foods I enjoyed. Since I no longer had a list of banned foods, I wasn't so bothered about eating them much anymore!

Although there were definite wobbles with my relationship with food, I lost almost all the weight by the time I got pregnant with my daughter nine months later. My body went back to my pre-pregnancy shape and I ate and exercised without rules and restriction again. That pregnancy was different, it wasn't risky, I was able to exercise and I didn't have any cravings or food aversions. Since I felt more in control, I gained a "normal" amount of pregnancy weight, which I easily lost afterwards. Having two children under two helped with that, of course!

Two more miscarriages and then a high risk

pregnancy full of issues resulted in my fabulous identical twin girls and also a body I didn't recognise – stretch marks, cellulite, droopy boobs and a stomach that had so many lines it reminded me of a Tube map. Knowing that I didn't want my children – especially my daughters – to learn about dieting, I decided to fix my body with that old fallback I had always relied on – exercise. What I didn't know then is that over-exercising the core area too soon after pregnancy causes problems and I ended up with diastasis recti, a condition where the tummy muscles don't come back together after pregnancy and so bulge out. Physio helped a little, but I was left with a protruding tummy amongst my other body changes.

I threw myself into staying busy – I became class rep for my daughter's nursery class, joined the PTA, became a volunteer director for a charity, went back to work as a nurse, started up a part-time business as personal trainer for women who couldn't go to gyms and studied to be a life coach and NLP practitioner. I would be at the weight-lifting gym before commuting to work three times a week. I was the queen of busy. If I didn't stop, I didn't have to think about how unhappy and how unattractive I was. I was a UK size six to eight and although I had strong arms, back and legs, the other post-baby parts that were stretched, saggy, marked and lined made me hide my body away. I stayed as busy as I could, always striving to achieve more and do more.

Fast forward to May 2016 when a group of ladies and I decided to do a thirteen-mile extreme obstacle course event. Training for it meant a stronger grip on my diet and exercise again, although I didn't realise it at the time. I was the fittest and strongest I had ever been when we started the race, not bad for a forty-something mother of four. The point of the event was teamwork – everyone was in teams and everyone in the event helped each other. Soon after the start we had the obstacle of a wall to climb over. Someone in front of me asked me if I wanted a leg up. I'm short, so was grateful of the offer. The thing was, he was a big strong man and I was a tiny little thing and I ended up being catapulted over the wall! I landed awkwardly on both legs, felt my knee hurt slightly and waited for the rest of my team, thinking the short rest would help. When they realised I couldn't actually put my foot to the floor, they carried me off to the side and I got whisked away to hospital.

Before I knew it, I had been admitted into a bed, taken off for a CT scan and had my leg in a contraption to stop it moving.

I'll never forget the look on the surgeon's face when he told me how serious my injuries were, that I would need surgery urgently and he didn't know when or if I'd walk again. My son had broken his leg when he was a toddler, had a full leg cast on for six weeks and fully recovered. "How hard could this really be?" I remember thinking. "Stick me in a cast, give me some crutches and let me go home. Do you know how busy I am?"

I looked around at the team of staff with the consultant all standing at the end of my bed, all with very serious looks on their faces. I know that look, after twenty years as a nurse, I'd given that same look to patients and relatives over the years. I didn't take it in, not when more doctors with serious faces came to see me, not when I was consented for surgery, not when I woke up in immense pain and an even bigger contraption on my leg, not even when the surgeon explained exactly how much metal was now inside my skin and how many bones broke and how he removed the shattered knee cap, not even when the physio suggested I set up a bedroom downstairs in my house. You see, I was BUSY and had too much to do!

All of a sudden, I wasn't busy anymore. My twenty-year nursing career was over – even if I'd been able to do my job from a wheelchair, I wouldn't have been able to commute! I lost part of my identity; I was bed bound with little control over the food I was being given and without any ability to move. In the past I had always fixed myself by controlling food or exercise or both and now I couldn't do that anymore. I had to release the control and I had to accept help to do nearly everything.

I was studying to become a Health Coach and this was when I learned to meditate. My mentor during the course started each session with some breathing exercises and a short meditation. Whilst I really wasn't into it and could barely do twenty seconds before my mind wandered off, I had plenty of time on my hands to practice and nothing to lose. I learned all I could about mindset and changing beliefs and I finally started using the NLP techniques I'd learned previously. I set out to walk again and love this body of mine, whatever state it was in, taking it one day at a time. It was a painful process (both physically and mentally). I started off with four different types of pain medication, including morphine. I couldn't even do the first exercises and I'd often cry or get angry in despair. I made very, very slow progress, often feeling like I was taking two steps forward and one step back. Figuratively speaking, of course – I wasn't taking steps anywhere!

Two operations later, three new scars and thirteen months after that fateful May day I was finally discharged from physiotherapy and I was able to walk without any aids. I'd gone from bed bound to wheelchair to crutches. Whilst another operation set me back slightly, I progressed to one crutch and then a stick to wobbly unaided walking. If you saw me walking you would know something wasn't right but I was walking and I was doing it on my own.

When I had to give up the control over everything, I realised my control and busyness came from a place of not feeling good enough. I didn't feel that I was good enough in so many aspects of my life.

Being a mother to three girls has really highlighted

to me the need for them not to go through what I did – years of yo-yo dieting and exercising and decades of being ashamed and hating my body. I don't want any woman to go through that, to feel that she isn't good enough. I now know that I AM enough, just as I am, scars and all.

My journey to "love thy body" is something I practice. I no longer hide my body in shapeless clothes or cover my scars in summer. I don't love every aspect of my body every day and there are some mornings when I feel bloated, my jeans feel tight or I have a bad hair day.

That's okay, I'm human and I'm perfectly imperfect. Three tips I'd like to share with you for helping you on your journey to loving YOURSELF would be:

Practice gratitude for your body – a simple sentence either said out loud or written in a journal. I felt pretty stupid doing this when I first started and now it's simply a daily habit I love to do. I also move my body in some way too.

Breathe – take a few minutes to shut off the world and just breathe. It really does quieten the inner chatter and can give you real clarity and a sense of peace. It doesn't have to be a full meditation, even just stopping and taking ten deep breaths can help.

Take time out – every day. EVEN when those busy days creep back in, I take some time out for myself in some way. It might be a quick meditation, a bubble bath with a glass of wine, a walk listening to a book or time in my gym. It might even just be having a hot cup of tea for five minutes before the school pick up. Every day. I can't be the best mum/wife/coach/friend if I haven't taken time for myself. It isn't selfish, it's essential.

My body grew and birthed four children, it enabled me to train for and complete a marathon despite being partially disabled, it allows me to express myself and reduce stress through movement, it enables me to dance around the kitchen with my kids. Even more simply, it takes me to where I need to go. Every scar and stretchmark and line and wobbly bit tells a story. My story. A story that needs to be told.

***

Claire Ashton is a Body Confidence Coach and Personal Trainer. She used mindset work, affirmations and visualisation as well as her vast experience in the healthcare setting to heal her mind and body after the trauma that years of dieting, several pregnancies and operations left on her body. She uses these skills to help other women love their bodies and increase their confidence so they can go out and live their lives to the fullest. Her mission is to help women be confident in their own skin so that they can step up to be seen, heard and successful – and she is also passionate about changing the dialogue so that future generations, like her daughters and their daughters, grow up in a society that is not ruled by the weight on the scales, or the size dress you can get into.

Facebook:
https://www.facebook.com/claireashtoncoaching
Instagram:
https://www.instagram.com/claireashtoncoaching
Website:
www.claireashton.co.uk

Don't Suffer in Silence

Claire Golinsky

So, this is my story. I'm not really sure where to start. My childhood was pretty good. I had loving parents, an older brother who I looked up to and a younger sister who I doted on.

But I was really shy, and this affected my life massively. I would get anxiety just walking down the road on my own. I thought it was just me being silly, that no one else felt this way and I needed to somehow snap out of it. But it was part of my life and it took me a long time to accept it.

In my teens, I discovered alcohol and I thought it was the answer to all my problems. After having a few drinks, I was no longer that shy timid girl who went bright red when someone so much as looked at her. I was now the life and soul of the party! And I loved it! So, I kept going out and spending all my money on alcohol. The only problem was, I didn't really have any money. So, I borrowed it. Then borrowed some more. First it was a credit card, and then it was personal loans. This debt of thousands of pounds was hanging over me everywhere I went. It started to weigh me down. It was all I could think about. Sadly, it didn't stop me drinking because that was my way of escaping the anxiety I felt. But I'd always go too far, and my nights out would end with me crying myself to sleep.

I couldn't tell anyone about my problems with money. I was deeply ashamed for getting into such a mess. So, I tried my best to ignore it and carry on. But the more I ignored it, the worse it got. On the inside I was feeling so low, I hated myself, but on the outside, I was fun Claire who was always up for a night out. Until one night, when I was out with my cousin and it all got too much. I didn't want to be here anymore; I couldn't see a way out. Everything was dark and I felt I only had one option. I'd convinced myself that I was such a massive disappointment to my family that this was for the best. I told my cousin that night, and even threatened to jump out of his flat window but seeing as we were both quite drunk he didn't take me seriously. He went to sleep, and I lay awake thinking of ways to do the unthinkable. I decided I would wake early before he woke and walk to the shops to buy paracetamol.

On my way back from the shops that morning, I somehow managed to take 80 tablets, a mixture of paracetamol and aspirin. When I look back now, it's clear how desperate I was. Did I want to die? Or was it a cry for help? I honestly don't know; all I know is it felt like my only way out. So, after taking an overdose, it turns out you don't just close your eyes and quietly die. Nope, your body will try and reject it, and for me, the rejection was awful. I was violently sick and felt so ill. I wouldn't allow my cousin to take me to hospital but agreed he could take me home and that I would come clean to my parents.

Thankfully I'm still here to tell the story but things could have been so different. It was a long journey of recovery after that and my parents did their best. They paid off my debts and found a way for me to pay them back gradually. But that, sadly, didn't fix my mental health.

I was told to find a counsellor so that I could talk about how I was feeling, but the one I found just made me feel worse by trying to find a bigger problem. This just made me feel my reason was not enough, so I stopped going. We continued with our lives, carrying on as if nothing had happened and my suicide attempt became an unspeakable subject. Apart from hiding all the tablets in the house and helping me sort the debt, my family didn't know what else to do. They assumed that what they were doing was the answer and I was magically all fixed. So, I tried to pretend I was. I don't blame them one bit, they had never had to experience anything like it before and it wasn't really talked about ten years ago.

I told myself I was selfish for feeling this way and I should be happy that I had a good life with a loving family. But deep inside I hated my life, the way I looked and spoke, just all of me. I always wished I was different, prettier, more confident, had a better job. I honestly felt like one big failure. Slowly but surely, I started to go downhill again. Yes, the debt seemed to be the reason for my depression before, but it just hid all the real reasons that I felt so low.

This part took me a while to write because it seems my brain blocked out the second overdose. I had to talk to my sister about it because she remembers a lot more than me. I'd been out drinking again, trying to escape the darkness in my head. I'd got home late when everyone was asleep, and I'd taken an overdose. Not as big as before and possibly a cry for help this time because I needed rescuing from what was happening to me. I messaged a friend to tell her what I'd done, she contacted my sister who came downstairs to confront me. All I remember was her anger. She was young and couldn't believe I'd be so selfish to think about leaving her. But she didn't understand that it wasn't personal and that at that moment in time all I could think about was making the pain go away. After the second time I was taken more seriously. My mum held me tight; I think it became real that one day I might succeed. Not really knowing what to do, she took me to the doctor. Thankfully she was amazing and helped me so much. She prescribed medication and helped me to talk about my feelings.

Life began to look much better. I quit drinking and I started volunteering for Samaritans as a listener. I decided I wanted to help people like me, help them to talk about their feelings without being judged. That no matter what is going on in your life that you have every right to express the way you feel and have support. Two years later and I was in a good place. I had spent a lot of time focusing on myself and discovering who I was. I still didn't love me, but I was accepting who I was. Things got even better when I met my future husband on a dating app. I fell madly in love and we were soon living together and getting married.

Then motherhood hit like a big train! It was all I wanted, to be married and start a family, but it was hard work! My daughter was perfect, but I wasn't prepared for the screaming and sleepless nights. Like most new mums, I pushed through and tried to be the best mum I could. Suddenly, I lost sight of me; I was Mum, and nothing else mattered. I was running on empty and my mental health started to suffer. I pushed it to the back of my mind because it wasn't about me anymore; all that mattered now was my daughter.

My marriage started to suffer, and my husband was feeling left out and alone. I felt I had to manage everything myself. Then, I found out I'd become pregnant again. After the initial shock, we came to terms with having another baby. We could do this. Until one day, when I was eleven weeks pregnant, I started cramping. I didn't worry too much at that point, I thought it was just part of pregnancy. But later that night I was in for a shock when I started bleeding.

I was alone; my daughter was six months old and my husband was at work. I knew I was losing my baby, but I had no idea what to do.

My husband came home early from work and we were seen by the doctor. He couldn't confirm either way and said we needed to wait to be scanned in the morning. The next day my worst fears came true. The scan revealed that my baby had died at six weeks and I was now miscarrying five weeks later. I was devastated. The staff were cold, as if I wasn't carrying an actual baby. I was sent home to miscarry.

Throughout the afternoon of New Year's Eve 2014 I went through horrendous cramps, bleeding and passing huge clots. Each time I rushed to the toilet I would wonder if that was my baby. I couldn't believe it was happening to me. I started to blame myself. I'd obviously done something wrong to make this happen. I must have had too much coffee or not enough water. Maybe I had eaten the wrong things. I went over it time and time again in my head, wondering what I could have done different. People started to avoid me. They didn't know what to say to me, but I felt so alone. I was grieving and still had a baby to take care of. It was a hard time for me. During that time, my husband felt pushed away again. I didn't know how to talk to him. It was like I was going through it all on my own. Our relationship suffered again, and I honestly didn't know if we'd get through it.

In time we tried to get back on track. I fell pregnant

with my son three months after the miscarriage, and although it wasn't planned, we battled through and made it work. This pregnancy was different to my first. I just couldn't enjoy it; I spent the first few months worrying that I would lose him. Towards the end I suffered with SPD and could barely walk. I took early maternity leave and spent my days trying to cope with the pain and look after a one-year-old. It was tough. In December, a week overdue, I was sent to hospital to be induced. After three failed attempts and hitting the forty-two weeks mark, I started to stress. My bump was huge and rock hard, it got to the point where I couldn't feel him move anymore. I was at my wits' end, crying constantly and begging them to do something. Finally, I had my waters broken. I remember them trying to give me an epidural in a dimly lit room whilst my contractions were shooting through me. My mum had to use the torch on her phone so that the anaesthetist could see what he was doing! Turns out it didn't work anyway! My son was struggling, his heart rate kept dropping, the alarm was raised about five times, each time a group of doctors/ midwives would rush in. It's safe to say I was scared. I managed to get to 10cm, but he wouldn't come out. So, I was rushed into theatre where I was put under general anaesthetic. A few hours later I groggily came around to find out I'd had a massive baby boy of 10lbs 1oz! I'd lost a lot of blood, had two blood transfusions and my baby boy had briefly stopped breathing. But, thankfully, everything turned out okay. That was until my mum fell in the car park outside and ended up in hospital with a broken pelvis.

I struggled massively with not having my mum by my side. I spent most days after the birth just crying. I was not only struggling with trying to manage with two babies, I needed my mum, and all I could think about was how much pain she must be in. When Aiden was nine days old, I travelled to the hospital with him to see my mum. I missed her so much and felt helpless and it'd happened two weeks before Christmas. I was so happy to find out she was going home on Christmas Eve. We were going to have Christmas together and it was the best present I could have asked for. Sadly, my mum will always suffer with ongoing pain from the accident but she's such an inspiration to me.

Fast forward eleven months. And I decided that I couldn't go through any more pregnancies or births. I had my two babies, so I had the implant inserted. Just over a month later I started bleeding. At first, I thought it must be my period, but something didn't seem right, so I did a pregnancy test, which came back positive. Suddenly, I was taken back to my miscarriage. I couldn't believe it was happening again; what did I do to deserve this? It felt like every time I started to get back on my feet something would come along to push me back down. I was scared. I went to the doctor who told me exactly what I had thought, I was having another miscarriage and to go home and wait it out. After a couple of days of bleeding and cramping I went back to the doctor who sent me for a scan, which revealed I had nothing in my womb, so I'd either miscarried already or it was ectopic. I'd heard of ectopic pregnancies before but didn't really know much about them. They did blood tests and sent me for an internal scan and there they found my baby growing in my right tube.

I remember the realisation hitting me, I'd lost another baby. But I put on a brave face and told people I wasn't sad because I hadn't known I was pregnant. In reality I was dying inside. I felt I had to keep it hidden because I wanted to make it easier for everyone else. I didn't want people avoiding me again, not knowing what to say. I was given three options. Surgery to remove my right tube and the ectopic, a series of injections to flush out the ectopic and possibly save the tube or keep having blood tests to see if the numbers went down. Sadly, I didn't get to choose. That night at around 1am I woke in the worst pain I had ever felt. My mum came over and my husband rushed me to hospital. I was violently sick in the car and kept passing out. It was so awful that I still get flashbacks now, four years on. Once in A&E I was hooked up and given morphine, but because it was busy, I was left behind. When they finally got me onto a ward, eight hours later, I felt a huge explosion inside. That moment will live with me forever because it was the moment I actually thought I was going to die. The doctor scanned me and confirmed my tube had ruptured and I was bleeding into my stomach.

I was rushed into theatre where they removed the tube along with the pregnancy. I lost a lot of blood and needed transfusions, but thankfully I lived to tell the tale. Sadly, it will always haunt me. I now had to recover from the trauma of what I'd just been through as well as come to terms with losing another baby. It took time but, if anything, it made me more determined. I could have lost my life but instead I'd been given another chance.

I started thinking about what I was passionate about in life, and decided it was time to use that passion and start my own business. My mum was my support; always there for me and helping me to make my dreams into reality.

In time I found myself again. I am still Mum, and I am proud to be called that, but I also get to be me too. I'm still on my journey to full self-love but I know I'm halfway there. If I wasn't me, I might not have survived everything I'd gone through. It's made me stronger. I've come to terms with my mental health issues, they won't go away but I know how to manage them. There will always be some days where I struggle to get out of bed and everything I do feels worthless, but I know it will pass and that I can get through anything. Always remember, be kind to yourself.

***

Claire is first and foremost a strong, independent woman passionate about helping others. She is mummy to Ciara and Aiden, her whole world, and wife to Ed.

She lives in Bedfordshire where she runs her business Eco Den from home.

She has decided to tell her story to reach out to others who may be struggling so they know they are not alone.

Her inbox is always open and you can reach her at:

www.facebook.com/clairehgolinsky
www.facebook.com/ecodenuk
www.instagram.com/ecodenuk
www.ecodenuk.com

Losing Weight Is NOT Your Life Purpose!

Danni Fraser

When I was young it was very normal to hate your body. It was typical to complain about the parts of your body you hated, to talk about what surgery you would have done to change the way you looked.

Honestly, it's heartbreaking to think that way because that negative self-talk didn't get me anywhere.

Now that's completely normal, celebrities are having surgery done all the time, boob jobs, Botox, tummy tucks, lip fillers, you name it. It's making women feel inferior and therefore are paying thousands to change the way they look. But it becomes an obsession; once they start, they can't stop and if you look at some celebrities, their face looks deformed and the surgery has aged them massively.

Why can't we just accept what we have been given?

It was also normal, and still is, to brag about losing weight, but it only makes you feel good for so long before you say, "but I still just want to drop one more dress size," or, "I've still got another stone to lose and then I will be happy."

How long will that happiness last?

Will you really be satisfied?

I wasn't.

Sometimes I would look back at old photos of when I claimed to be fat and think, "Gosh, I would give anything to be that size and look like that now!"

Have you ever thought that?

I have been every size from a size six to a size eighteen/twenty. Not one particular size made me happy. When I was a size six I was body shamed, told I looked pale and ill, people used to comment and say, "Have you even eaten today?" to which I would reply that I had, followed by another comment like, "Yeah, what did you eat, a biscuit?!"

You see, people who think they are fat are so desperate to lose weight yet skinny people can struggle just as much with insecurities and experience body shaming too, and many skinny people are desperate and struggling to put weight on.

So, me as a size eighteen/twenty, mum of three, there were so many times when I looked in the mirror and all I could see were my imperfections. My mum tum, my cellulite, my back rolls that disgusted me and sent the tears streaming down my face.

I was disconnected to my body, to the beauty, to what my body had been through with pregnancy and childbirth. I was so cruel to myself and I was completely broken.

I spent years allowing my dress size to determine my self-worth, crying in changing rooms because I had to size up. I felt lazy, I felt fat, I felt disgusting, and unlovable.

The only time I ever felt loved and wanted was in my teens because I was skinny, and I felt that attracted the lads to me. Even then I always compared myself to other girls like, "Why would he want me when he can have someone like her?"

When you're slim, people seem to look at you differently, do you find that?

Lose weight and you'll be praised like crazy!

Who are you losing weight for, though? Yourself? Or for others' approval?

Everything changed when I finally realised that I don't want to be skinny to like myself, for anyone else to love me or for anyone else's approval. I was done giving a fuck! I was fed up of living my life on other people's terms. I was so done with the scales and I chucked those bitches out a long time ago! I became obsessed with weighing myself daily, sometimes several times a day and it was always a make or break decision as to how I might feel, if I would accept and love myself that day. I was done with torturing myself.

I was fed up of telling myself 'I will be happy when...'

When what?

You lose more weight?

There is no when, there is only NOW!

The size of my jeans should not have to dictate how beautiful I feel, not today, not ever!

The problem is, when growing up, I never heard people saying positive affirmations like they do today. Those big bold statements like "I am beautiful, I am worthy, and I absolutely love my body."

I actually have to stop myself sometimes mid-sentence when I start apologising to people.

Why are we continuously apologising for the way we look?

"Sorry I look a mess today," as I rock up in my joggers or answer the door in my PJs.

"Sorry my hair is a mess," when I haven't slept in days because the baby had me up all night.

I have to remind myself that I have four kids and many hats to wear. I fight with my body constantly with this autoimmune disease that I was diagnosed with after the birth of my first daughter. Living with thyroid disease makes me want to sleep for a week and pretend I have no reason to get up in the mornings. The reality is, I have kids to take care of. Staying in bed and feeling sorry for myself is just not ever an option.

My thyroid controls my life, every emotion, my energy levels, my daily moods. Managing a home, four kids, and trying to run a business, it just consumes me most days. It has a habit of slowing me down so much and it's so damn frustrating. I just feel exhausted 24/7.

People, other women, they don't relate to perfection because perfect doesn't exist. They relate to what's real. They relate to your struggles because they feel them too.

I had to work on my mindset.

I learned that some people are just going to judge you regardless, and the greatest mental freedom is not giving a shit what others think.

I realised that just maybe people aren't judging me at all, maybe it's all in my mind…

I saw this quote and I was just like, "YES!"

"Confidence is silent and other people's insecurities are loud as fuck." I mean, how true is this?

The next time someone puts you down, just remember it says so much about the person that they are.

You just own who you are. You have to block out the noise.

Speaking of noise, social media has a lot to answer for too, doesn't it? It can be a positive thing to enable you to seek help, support, make connections, new friends, so many positives yet so many negatives too.

So summer is approaching, your social newsfeed is about to be flooded with women only showing their best bits, you feel shit because you didn't lose weight as you promised yourself ready for that bikini bod. Well, Danni's definition of a bikini body is, "Just put a bikini on your body and flipping well own it, lady!"

I had to change my mindset because I realised just

how much I was missing out on those special moments because of how disgusting I felt, because of my double chin, my back fat and my cellulite. The truth is my kids don't care what size my bikini is or that my cellulite shines in the sun. My kids just wanted me to be present in photos.

And now I refuse to sit out of photos with my kids in the summer or anytime really, and I am done hating myself for not having a slim figure or abs. I refuse to spend the rest of my life feeling trapped in my body, feeling completely and utterly shit about my photos being taken by other people or at the wrong angle.

You know, everyone is fighting their own battles, so I try not to judge. I just want to be that constant reminder for women to stop comparing, and I know that sounds easier said than done but what you see on social media is not reality. It's just a highlight reel.

Have you ever taken a photo and worry that it's not good enough? STOP, BACK UP AND DO NOT DELETE! You have to stop looking at the parts of your body you hate and love all of who you are. Your skin, it's not smooth. Your belly, it doesn't need to be flat. Your hair, it doesn't need to be brushed and well-groomed and you don't have to look like the women you have just stalked on your social media, because they don't even look like that!

Stop comparing yourself, your body, your life when you're scrolling your newsfeed, because lighting; angles; poses; editing; all can easily alter how a person looks, and I know this because I spent so long practicing. Over time, we learn how to take great photos, especially with technology these days, it's so easy to add filters, to take photos at your best angles.

All sides of who we are, are beautiful, ladies. You are worthy of knowing, finding and loving you and all of your thousands of layers. Just please believe and know you are enough.

I mean, can you imagine having to feel like you have to prove yourself every day, no matter what you're wearing or doing?

Makeup or no makeup.

Size ten or a size twenty.

Semi-naked or fully clothed.

Honestly, it gets tiring.

MY FOURTH PREGNANCY

This is the time that I finally fell in love with my body. This is where the journey truly began.

Does that sound a bit cringy? A bit cocky, even?

"OMG, she is so in love with herself!"

"She's so self-obsessed!"

My previous three pregnancies, all I could think about was how would I lose the weight, how quickly could I make it happen and get my body back? After my first two pregnancies I lost the weight quite quickly because I had already been slim before pregnancy, so

I never really had to try so hard. After my third, it was a little harder and it took much longer, and I started to hate my body so much more.

Somehow, somewhere, I lost my way with my self-love journey and I had to work so goddamn hard to reconnect again.

Maybe you can relate.

Pregnancy, you see it as an end to so many things. The end of your body as you once knew it, the end of feeling confident, the end of looking like all the other women and the end to wearing bikinis and nice clothes, but little do you know… it's just the beginning.

It's the beginning of something beautiful!

Pregnancy with my fourth, something in me changed. I had spent a few years already on my self-love journey and this time I didn't want to feel like I had done in previous pregnancies.

I said, "This time I'm going to appreciate my body, accept my body is changing and it's growing a beautiful little human. My body is incredible!" It's the first time I felt amazing in pregnancy where I couldn't wait to show off my bump at any given opportunity and you know what? This time not once did I worry about my weight or worry about losing weight after birth, this time I just truly embraced it all.

If I could get through and survive childbirth, I sure as hell can get through this shit of learning to love my body and myself more. I'm so PROUD of the work I've put in over the years into loving every inch of my body.

Actually, sharing my body in pregnancy was the part of my journey where I finally became confident and brave enough to share my photos, laid bare. Not naked naked, just in my lingerie.

I had no shame. I had accepted myself just as I was. That takes patience, time, kindness to yourself, positive affirmations often and a whole lot of gratitude.

Honestly, it's just wonderful, it's a sign of relief when you no longer care what anyone thinks. That freedom is like no other. Being completely free in your skin, stripping yourself bare... Real and raw. It feels so good to empower another woman to feel confident in her skin and bring back some reality into the world. The only way my daughters were going to grow up confident in their bodies was for me to be confident in mine. My eldest daughter has already struggled from the age of nine with self-confidence, but we worked on that, and I honestly believe it's because I made sure I never talked negatively about my body in front of her. Now she's a teenager, and we have the world of social media, she's definitely finding self-acceptance harder.

However, I can definitely see change; I can see it all over my social media that more women are starting to appreciate and respect their bodies. There is more self-love. A lot of you may not be quite there yet and that's okay, it will take time, but I hope you learn to love yourself and your body eventually.

Don't get me wrong, I don't love my body all the time, I still have those "ugh" moments, but now it's just for a moment. I use my tools to help me when I'm feeling not so 'myself'.

It's taken seven long years in total of hard work. You don't just wake one morning and decide to love yourself. It's a process, it's a journey, and it's a positive one!

One day at a time, ladies.

One positive affirmation each day.

One kind compliment to yourself.

Whatever your size, you are size beautiful.

Your weight may fluctuate, but never your worth.

Respect yourself, respect your body and inhale that self-love.

When you finally commit to your journey of self-love, it's massive, it's a huge step.

You have to commit fully to loving your body right now, though, just as it is, in all its glory!

Be grateful to wake up every day in this beautiful body of yours that keeps you alive.

The journey is hard.

The journey is long.

The journey will make you, break you, and sometimes it will test you, but you will eventually find the freedom that you never even knew existed, and only then will you find self-acceptance.

Honestly, life is too short wasting another day at war with yourself. Start learning to love the woman you are becoming. If you think that self-acceptance and self-love is only if you look a certain way, you are in for self-destruction! Say it loud to yourself right now: "I will no longer strive for perfection and I will learn to love myself, just as I am."

Take off the mask you wear on social media and experience something really special, where you are just YOU! Authentically YOU! You start to be real and raw and unapologetically YOU! When you stop trying to be perfect for everyone, when you step out of your comfort zone, when you step out into the real world and you say, "This is me and this is who I am."

Honestly, it's just so liberating.

It's much harder trying to be someone else, trying to be someone you're not, and eventually you'll get caught out trying to be yourself!

So, here's my biggest tips:

I unfollowed hundreds of picture-perfect women on my Instagram.

Listen to Christina Aguilera's song "Beautiful" and I mean really listen to the lyrics, watch the music video, because they are both so powerful and so relatable.

Write down all the awful things you have ever said to yourself, about your body, and burn it. Then commit to stop the negative self-talk.

Buy some affirmation cards and pick a new one each day. Say it over and over again. Keep using them until you really start to believe in what you're saying. Yes, at first you will feel silly, but honestly, they work! If you work on your mindset, if you get the inside right, the outside will fall into place.

Be everyone's biggest cheerleader, all the women on your social media. Clear out all the negative Nancys, so you are left with everyone who makes you feel good, people who inspire you. Hype up all the girls and tell them how beautiful they are, but most of all, tell yourself.

Be kind to you, I'm rooting for you, and you know that little girl inside of you… she has been rooting for you too, this whole damn time!

***

Danni is thirty-four, lives in Oxfordshire UK and is a mum of four.

Her mission is to create a generation of fierce women, to make every woman feel worthy, to help women heal and to remind them they are so much more than a number on their jeans.

From Crutches to Catwalk

Hannah Westbrook-Bryan

It was a Saturday morning, and I was thirteen years old, I left my friend's house to cross the road to get my coat from my house as we were going to go to Milton Keynes shopping…

I woke up in the Luton and Dunstable hospital a few days later with the worst headache in the world; I had no idea what was going on! Turns out I got knocked down by a car, when I say knocked down, I was actually flung twenty feet further up the road… We lived on a hill!

I broke my hip and had head injuries and was rushed to the Royal Free hospital in London by police escort. It is only now that I realise how serious this actually was. BUT the lady that knocked me down didn't get breathalysed or charged as there were no witnesses, her word against mine, and I (luckily) have no memory of the event, just the memories of what followed.

After stiches in my head, and an operation on my hip, I had to have a metal clamp attached to my hip for it to mend, and I was discharged from hospital. I wasn't allowed to put my foot to the ground and faced walking with crutches for at least six months. I arrived home to lots of friends popping in to see me, they brought flowers, cards, chocolates, etc… it was lovely. Even the local vicar came to see me.

But I was housebound, I was lonely. There was no one home during the day, I literally had to stay in my bedroom 24/7 and I hated it. I didn't get to complete my county trials for tennis, which I loved and was actually good at (sport wasn't my strong point)! I felt so alone with just the telly to keep me company. Back then I had a black and white telly, with a dial… I had to get out of bed, grab my crutches and hobble to the telly to turn the dial to choose one of the four channels that we had available back then! I remember being so frustrated one day that I bum shuffled down the stairs holding my crutches and went to walk down the hill to meet some friends from school. I got caught by my stepdad (bloody home early that day) and got told off! During this time, I don't ever remember crying, I'm not sure how I dealt with my emotions back then, I just felt very very alone.

Yay! I was allowed to go to school… But I had to be dropped off at reception by my mum in the car. Trust me, when you are on crutches a Ford Capri is a very tough vehicle to get in and out of, especially when you are feeling like a hindrance and are conscious that your mum is always in a rush and running late, work was always very important! I was left in this room by myself by the main entrance, again alone a lot of the time. I wasn't allowed to go many places around the school in case someone bumped into me and knocked me over. School work was delivered to me, when teachers remembered. My saving grace was set six English, a small group of children that had their class in the room I was in and I could join in and interact with people.

Gradually I managed to get my freedom back, I was able to get around better with my crutches. I went shopping for the first time with my mum and gran (the most inspirational person I will ever meet), but we had to get a wheelchair from shop mobility. Using the crutches to get around was just too much hard work, but still I felt like I was a fraud. I shouldn't have needed the wheelchair, there were people out there that had an actual need for one, so I didn't go shopping again, at least not until I didn't need aids for support.

After about two months, I was able to go out and meet my friends but was still at this point using crutches, although once at someone's house I could usually hobble around without them. A group of us used to hang out at my boyfriend's house; to be honest, I couldn't quite work out why he was with me. I mean, I wasn't the prettiest girl at school or very popular. He always had money and the latest things, and I didn't. This one day we were all at his house and he wanted to talk to me, so we went to the bathroom, he locked the door and basically gave me an ultimatum, a choice of two sexual acts. I figured I couldn't run away, so I had no choice but to have sex with him. We had had sex once before, so I figured it was the easier option. A few days later, I tried to tell the girls who I thought were my friends, they laughed and asked why would he do that? I felt embarrassed and stupid, why did I bother saying anything in the first place? I never spoke of it again and carried on being his girlfriend as though nothing had happened. I didn't ever tell my mum, out of fear of being told off and shouted at.

As I got fitter and was able to join in with classes as I no longer need the crutches, I started taking part in PE again. But I felt very self-conscious of my scar. It's a seven-inch scar that runs down the outside of my right leg, my PE skirt didn't cover it and I felt everyone staring at it. I hated it, it was still very red and very prominent on my milky white legs. I asked my mum to write me a letter so I could wear jogging bottoms, which thankfully I was allowed. After a few months, my PE teacher shouted out in the changing rooms, "You still not ready to wear a PE skirt yet?" Everyone stared at me, I wanted the ground to swallow me up, as let's face it everyone had forgotten what had happened by this point. Luckily, I only have the scar and the memories of being at home, I don't actually remember the accident itself, only what I have been told. I was knocked twenty feet up the road, unconscious. When I came around, I punched the person that was trying to put an oxygen mask on me, and I think I might have sworn! I do remember seeing one of my friends in the hospital, and telling them they could have my headache.

During this whole period, I didn't have any counselling, it was just assumed I would get on with it, so I did.

We started going to an under eighteens disco on a Tuesday night at Ritzy in Dunstable. I always went with my friend as my mum wouldn't take us, she always had things to do. It was fashionable to wear skimpy hot pants and tiny bra tops, which I felt very self-conscious in. I borrowed an outfit from my friend but wore thick black tights to hide my scar, which I pretty much did until much later on in life. My scar didn't really fade until I went away to the Dominican Republic when I was nineteen and the sun bleached it. Even then, I still didn't really wear anything too revealing and was still very conscious of my figure.

I had a big falling out with my mum and stepdad when I was sixteen and moved out to live with my dad, who I didn't really know. He hadn't really been a figure in my life growing up, but I had nowhere else to go, all my friends still lived at home! My freedom had been taken away from me, I no longer had a door key so couldn't come and go as I pleased like I could at my mum's, but then they were hardly ever there so I needed a key, I guess. I'd go out clubbing with my friends and Dad would have to get up and let me in at 4am! I honestly don't know why I wasn't allowed a key, I was sixteen, working full time and paying keep. I guess my dad didn't really know how to deal with a child being at home, as I hadn't lived with him since he left when I was very little.

At twenty-one, I moved out. I moved in with my friend Marc and we had a fabulous few years together. He was renting a flat but then bought a place and I just moved in with him. We had such a laugh and I have so many great memories from these times, nights out, parties, Christmas meals with our friends, we were Luton's version of Will and Grace! Or at least I thought we were.

I had finally stopped being so self-conscious about my scar, but I still had issues and became more focused on my weight and the overall way I looked. When I was in my early twenties working in recruitment, I just thought I was FAT, so I ate very little. I would go a whole day without food some days. I went to fitness classes, proud of myself that I found I liked circuit training. I was happy, but I was very skinny, I was a size eight and thought I felt amazing.

One way or another I have always struggled with my weight, never being able to really stick to anything like healthy eating, always going through stages of eating lots (not always the right things) and eating hardly anything. I was always under the impression that not eating meant I lost weight and that was when I felt at my best, or so I thought. Over the years, I have been very up and down about my weight. I was what I thought was chunky at school, to not caring what people thought to feeling fat and starving myself. I have been a size eight and felt amazing about myself, flat tummy, etc... and then I have been as big as a fourteen and at 5'3 I just felt dumpy. I didn't know about nutrition, no one really explained the benefits of a healthy diet and regular exercise, so it was a case of all or nothing at some points.

It is only now that I am in my forties that I realise, with the help of so many wonderful women I have met these last few years, especially Love Thy Body Project, that I won't be the same dress size in every shop, and that's okay. I might not have a flat belly like I used to, but I have two very healthy children, and it's thanks to them I actually now have boobs!

Having a daughter, I am very conscious of the fact that I don't ever want her to overthink the way she looks or worry about her size. She is a typical twelve-year-old, always knows what is best, so too much sugar and not enough water is her answer. We are changing that, though, and she seems willing.

Three years ago, I agreed to take part in a body positive catwalk. I had no idea what it would entail but never in my life did I think it would be modelling underwear! I picked the biggest pair of knickers from the collection I could, and there I was standing on stage in my Bridget Jones knickers feeling amazing and thinking how brave the other ladies were in their stockings and thongs... That moment when Annie (forever grateful it was her and not me going first) walked on stage in her underwear and the venue erupted with cheers and whistles, that was the moment I was proud to be standing here with these ladies supporting body positivity. Being comfortable in my own skin didn't happen overnight, but this was definitely the start of my self-love journey. I then accepted a challenge and with five other ladies and our daughters in Devon, we entered a body positive photoshoot. A cold day in March on Slapton Sands in our bikinis and wellies, we came third in the national competition. Fast forward to early 2020 I was lucky enough to be chosen to do the catwalk again, but this time I promised myself I would go for a thong, and I did and felt amazing. Now my body hadn't changed much at all, I still have my mum tum, but I have worked a lot on my mindset, by reading books, other people's journeys, having gratitude and making sure I practiced it daily. Listening and learning from others has helped me to be happy with me, confident in my appearance, regardless of what size I am.

***

Hannah is now a thriving businesswoman living life on her terms. She is based in the South-West of England where she lives with her husband, two children and their handsome rescue pup. Hannah is passionate about helping others and is a Leader for Mums In Business International where she empowers women daily. She is also CEO of Willow PR where she helps other small business owners with a variety of admin-related tasks to enable them to grow their business and follow their passions without having to worry about the small behind-the-scene details.

You can connect with Hannah at:

https://www.facebook.com/Willowprva
www.instagram.com/willowpr.pa

Low Tide

Helen Ingham

"Where are you? You got off the train twenty minutes ago, you should be in the car by now."

"I don't know. We've taken a wrong turn coming out of the station and we're lost. I can't see my mum's car. We're walking under a bridge and there's a bloke following us."

"Yeah, whatever. Fucking lying bitch."

Cue a police car pulling alongside us, informing us we were in the red-light district and taking us safely to the other side of Piccadilly station where my parents were waiting frantic in the car. Therein lies the lightbulb moment when I realised that I did not want to be that person, that I was worth more and that I would not put up with it any longer.

As a child I was skinny and awkward, yet I found it easy to find friends and social environments never fazed me. Growing up in the nineties meant social media wasn't a thing and my childhood was spent like many others watching cartoons, playing out until the sun set and enjoying the simple things that children take for granted. My upbringing was good; I came from a stable family home and was lucky enough to enjoy privileges that many others don't – including a private education, which although I hated provided me with opportunities I only see now as an adult.

I never felt like I fitted into the grammar school mould. My years there were overshadowed by a constant desire to be like other people who seemingly had it all. Around the age of fourteen I began to rebel – skipping school, underage drinking, (very mild) recreational drug use, promiscuity... the types of things that signal a total lack of self-esteem. The more I attempted to be one of the 'cool girls', the less it felt like I was accepted. My desire to prove myself came to dizzy heights when at fourteen nearly fifteen I got myself a boyfriend a couple of years older than me. Thinking he was the dog's bollocks, I bragged about it and went out of my way to spend as much time with him as possible at the detriment of my education, my mental health and my social life at a time where I should have been enjoying being a teen.

It didn't take long for the red flags to appear. Over the course of the next two to three years I would experience emotional abuse behind closed doors that I never dared to speak of. At the time I was oblivious to it; in my young naivety all I could see was attention and the thrill of drama, a fucked-up love story in which I would become the main character.

There is so much I don't remember about those

lost years; I succeeded in creating the ultimate black box in my subconscious, a dark Pandora's box where I would immediately push all thoughts and memories of trauma. The flashbacks are hypnagogic yet disturbingly real, despite the fact time can twist and distort memories, and I occasionally relive them like screenshots of a past life: the gun aimed at me after I kissed a male friend in the pub, the threat of aiming the gun at said male friend, being spat on in my face as he pulled up alongside me when stalking me on my birthday night out, the samurai sword he owned thrown at a full pop bottle inches away from my body, which caused it to explode like my brain wanted to, the painkillers he swallowed one by one until I was forced to admit to something I hadn't done to satisfy his ego, the phlegm I was forced to suck out of his nose to prove that I loved him, the cold feet and smell of beer upon his return from a club at midnight whilst I had been left in his bedroom so he knew exactly where I was, the threat of being watched and monitored every hour of the day as far as an isolated farmhouse in Spain on holiday with my parents, being led to a park bench by older girls whom he had instructed to 'scare the shit out of me' until I again admitted to something I had not done – so many times in those years was I goaded to tell a truth which was actually a lie, resulting in the loss of friends who believed his twisted stories. Gaslighting. The holes in the wall from his anger, the blanket on the floor I was made to sleep on like a dog whilst he slept in his bed next to me, the graffiti on his bedroom wall, which he would regularly top up with other girls' names. But he never touched me. I never had a bruise or mark on my physical body to prove what he was doing to my mind. Years later, I would come to understand that although I was no saint, I hadn't deserved any of that. Nobody ever deserves treatment like that.

The day I found myself receiving abuse for getting innocently lost in the busy city centre was the day I decided I was done. His emotional abuse was no longer going to control me, so I called it off. Following this came a proposal ("Please don't leave me!"), a few more stalking incidents ("I can see you in the park with your mates, I'm watching.") and eventually many years later a brief apology in a direct message on social media, which I ignored before blocking him. I had let go but it would be a long time before I forgave myself and I am still waiting for the mental scars to fade completely.

Then came the best years – my glorious late teens and twenties with all the energy, collagen, lack of responsibility and fun I deserved.

Work.
Eat.
Party.
Repeat.

I found love in myself and my wonderful husband whom I married in my late twenties. Life was better than good, it was euphoric. Gone was the lost girl who undervalued herself, in her place had grown a confident, happy adult with admirable morals and a positive mental attitude that would shine from my pores. I grew up and settled down in a life that fifteen-year-old me had dreamed of.

But life is such that the sun cannot always shine. Even the stars must hide behind clouds now and again. Happiness and contentment can ebb and flow like the tide, and when the waves retreat to a rough ocean one must look for the pattern left in the wet sand for answers until it is time for the gentle water to return.

Becoming a mother defined my adult life. It simultaneously broke me and made me; my most feared weaknesses and vulnerability versus the strength and resilience I worked so hard to develop. The moment I became 'Mum' is the one that made me who I am today.

At thirty-one we welcomed our first child into the world; a daughter who gave us so much joy. Of course, it was challenging learning to adapt to motherhood and winging it to a new normal, but it was amazing. I adored her and she fitted straight into our little family bubble. She gave me a sense of fulfilment and purpose as it became clear that I was good at being a mother despite it taking around four months to feel that unconditional bond and rush of love they say you feel immediately at birth when they are placed in your arms. I had spent a decade learning to love myself and figure out who I was, only for this to be turned on its head as I lost myself again to who this tiny human needed me to be. Glimmers of me were still there and I was by no means resentful or sad about it, but it is true that parenthood inevitably changes you. It must, to a certain degree, in order to survive that first year of newborn challenges.

During pregnancy I watched my body in awe as it grew and adapted to fit a 7lb baby. Being small and slight framed I felt heavy (I confess I did put on three stone due to all the donuts) and uncomfortable. I never developed any stretchmarks or permanent changes aside from the loose 'mum tum' and thread veins on my legs. I hate my legs, but I love my tiny boobs, which grew an extra cup size after having children. My pelvic floor is the only part of me left destroyed beyond repair after bringing two children into the world; I cannot sneeze or jump without wetting myself and find it devastating to be resigned to super plus size tampons once a month. But despite the changes to my body, I have nothing but the utmost respect for what it has been through and enabled me to do, I love my post-baby body even if bodycon dresses are now way beyond my comfort zone.

Then ding-ding, round two! Just two and a half years later we were blessed with a second child, a son who although was planned for, arrived in my womb a little earlier than we had counted for given that the toddler was already a full-time job.

The pregnancy hit me like a ton of bricks. It was so different to my first. From the beginning something was off – I wasn't excited or nervous, I just pretended to be since that is what everyone expects, isn't it? Inside I was becoming numb. Every day felt like going through the motions, each one a step closer to him arriving into the world and me feeling like myself again, only this was not going to be as simple as I hoped. I was becoming unravelled and my perfect little life was spiralling with my unsettled mind.

Baby boy arrived happy and healthy after a straightforward birth; it wasn't until he was around two months old that we started to notice that he wasn't well, which was then followed by a ten month battle, including eight different health professionals, leading to a diagnosis of severe reflux. At the time of examination his nasal passage and throat were so blocked and damaged from acid that they couldn't get the camera through during the endoscopy. Meanwhile, whilst we spent his first months trying to convince doctors that there was a problem, we endured hell at home. There is a reason that sleep deprivation is used as a form of torture in some cultures. Averaging a couple of hours per night, I truly believe that this was the trigger for my own diagnosis of postnatal depression.

During the pregnancy and the months after delivery, I became lost in the corridors of my own mind. Finding it increasingly harder to function day by day, the signs and symptoms of PND were there but I kept it to myself. The best way I can describe my brain at the time is this: do you remember seeing the images in the wake of the 9/11 terror attacks where pieces of paper silently drifted through the smoke and dust, coming to settle on the rubble that littered the pavement below? That was the visual image of inside my head. My thoughts became tangles in a labyrinth that I would have to find my own way out of. Concentration was non-existent; I couldn't string a sentence together, even though I knew somewhere inside what I was trying to verbalise. It was as though there was a barrier between my head and body which prevented me from speaking any logic. Lack of sleep meant that I was mentally and physically exhausted – my bones ached from my crown to my toes, a type of lethargy that I imagine must follow intense illness. Being a petite UK size eight, I watched as my collarbone began to show through my skin and the elastic which held my underwear around my hips became loose; it wasn't that I intentionally starved myself, I just wasn't hungry. Personal hygiene became a daily choice, I would usually favour dry shampoo and a spray of deodorant simply because I didn't have the strength in my arms to lift the hairdryer or the energy to stand in the shower. There were days when I would make it to evening before realising that I had forgotten to brush my teeth. I was emotionally numb; void of any feelings

– not sad, not anxious, not overwhelmed, just nothing. Quite literally, the lights were on but there was nobody at home. Mists of rage would engulf me from nowhere and I'd find myself erupting at the smallest thing to a point that I was ashamed once the fog subsided. Guilt crept in and made itself at home, nestling itself in the corners of my mind. It felt like my once happy marriage was crumbling as I became a burden to my husband who was desperately trying to keep us afloat.

Amidst my battle with PND, one of my oldest friends was very suddenly diagnosed with cholangiocarcinoma, a liver cancer that would devastatingly claim his thirty-four-year-old life in a matter of just sixty-one days, leaving a four-year-old daughter and his wife behind, who is also one of my best friends. It was another huge trauma to deal with on top of my already fragile mind and one which tipped me over the edge of sanity. I accepted defeat and screamed for help.

Healing starts with a long, hard, look in the mirror. First, you have to accept the person that stares back at you, owning each of the mistakes you've made, forgiving yourself for them, vowing to become a better person, which in turn leads to the motivation to move forward. Face your demons instead of running from them, otherwise you'll never truly be free. Without self-acceptance, one cannot arm oneself with the personal knowledge it takes to move forward – only you know what you want from your life, what your goals are. Living a lie can't help you find yourself and unaddressed traumas have a nasty habit of coming back to bite you in the arse. Don't bottle things up, open your black box every now and again. Had I had the courage to do this myself much earlier on in life then perhaps I would not still question whether there is a link between the abuse I suffered and developing postnatal depression – was my mind not strong enough because it was still full of shadows?

Once I found my motivation and was ready to start finding myself again, I made small steps and educated myself about the condition, reaching out to others who had experienced the same and being brave enough to talk about it with close family members. Antidepressants were prescribed, which a year down the line I swear by. I weaned myself off them too early during the pandemic and had an anxiety relapse, which told me I needed to be kinder to myself and go slower. Gradually I began to make more time for myself and fall back in love with the little things that made me, me – working, cooking, shopping, seeing friends and writing became more like therapies than hobbies (although I did get myself a fabulous therapist who helped to encourage me through darker days). Small triumphs were found in daily activities, such as applying make-up or dressing in an outfit that wasn't pyjamas. Slowly but surely the light crept back in and I regained parts of myself that I had forgotten all about, parts that I had liked.

I will never get over the fact that I was robbed of the joy I should have felt bringing my son up in those early days, the last chance I will get at the newborn bubble, but I am at peace with how far I've come.

Time has taught me that I am not alone in my life experiences, but certain subjects are still taboo and unspoken where they should be normalised and discussed freely without a sense of judgement. These 'dirty secrets'; abuse, grief, mental health, medication, etc. are rarely shared on the square panels of social media which hide revelations and half-truths that society deem distasteful if admitted in public. "Don't air your dirty laundry!" my grandma would have said. Yet personally I found my love/hate relationship with social media to be my salvation in the form of like-minded, non-judgemental parents who understood the position I found myself in. There is always somebody else out there who gets it, but you often have to ask for the support. Reach out. There is no shame in trying to understand yourself, nor in acceptance of who you really are.

So, who am I now? I'm still figuring that out, but I can tell you that the version of myself which has appeared in my thirty-fifth year is the truest one yet. Now, I love myself first – I had to for the sake of my children and husband, otherwise there wouldn't have been a 'me' left for them. Between writing, holistic therapies and speaking out unashamedly, I am proof that you can survive and rebuild after trauma. More than that, I am proof that you can be happy after the storm passes.

True, there is likely going to be another storm down the line, the climate hasn't totally changed just yet, but with the courage, strength and knowledge I have accumulated through the turbulence of previous years I have the confidence to say, "This too shall pass."

***

Helen lives in Greater Manchester with her husband and two children. Writing lesson plans and resources for teachers by day, she is also an author with her debut novel *Cold Coffee: Spilling the tea on the things nobody tells you about parenting* due for release in late February 2021, in which she candidly shares the highs and lows of her own bumpy journey through motherhood and the things she wishes she had been told beforehand. Following her experience with post-natal depression and maternal mental health, she is an avid supporter of normalising the subject and breaking stigmas attached to this by speaking out honestly and openly, whilst attempting to educate, encourage and empower the community with a touch of humour through her words. She wings her way through life and parenting with her mantra "This too shall pass", with the support of some good quality gin.

To contact please follow her social media pages:

Facebook:
https://www.facebook.com/coldcoffee34

Instagram:
https://instagram.com/cold_coffee85

I've Always Been Thin

Jane Hill

I've always been thin. And my dear mum, who died last December aged ninety-eight, was always very worried about me. My dad was 6ft tall and thin, and my mum, at 5ft 6in, was slim too, but despite this, she worried incessantly about me and my eating habits.

I'm an only child, born when my mum and dad were thirty-six and forty-six respectively, so I suppose it's not surprising that my mum worried about me. She was quite an anxious person, though far more outgoing than I am and I understand now that she found in me a huge focus for her anxiety that she hadn't had before. The anxiety was just hanging around, if you like, waiting for something to fix on. Don't get me wrong, she and Dad loved me, and I them, but the anxiety was there before me, I see that now.

I had a happy, quiet, comfortable childhood and benefited from what you might call benign neglect. I had, and took for granted, what every child deserves to have – I was fed, clothed, warm, secure and loved. I had friends, I had toys, and, most importantly, books.

At school, I learned to read so fast that the teacher ran out of books for me to learn with and I was far ahead of the rest of the class. We lived on the edge of countryside, so it was easy to just disappear for hours with my friends and just come home when we felt like it, after playing in the fields behind the house. Dad was a solicitor, Mum a doctor's daughter, so we had a comfortable, unostentatious life – not super-wealthy, but not poor.

Looking back now, I can see that, whereas my mum's anxiety probably circled the usual practical considerations – was I warm enough, properly dressed, had I done my homework? – until I was about ten or twelve, her concerns began to change after that. I grew taller and much, much skinnier, and, embarking on those difficult teenage years, much more resentful of my mum's concerns that I was eating enough. Mealtimes, especially when eating out (not that we did that very much, except on holiday), became very fraught, and I found food and eating less and less appealing. At this point too, Mum was in her fifties, menopausal, I now realise, and becoming anxious about swallowing – she actually told me very recently that this had been a great problem for her at this time of life. What I found fascinating about her telling me was that she clearly hadn't realised I knew already – but I think that's another story.

So, eating was an unhappy activity, deeply uncomfortable, with an anxious, menopausal mother and a sensitive teenager who just wanted to be left alone to nibble whatever took her fancy on the plate who felt, as she saw it, mercilessly nagged at every mealtime to eat a bit more. And the more Mum tried, as she undoubtedly saw it, to encourage me to eat, the more unhappy and upset I became. Dad occasionally pointed out that if I were given smaller helpings I might get on better, or that I should be left to eat what I wanted, but I think that he mostly stayed out of this unhappy battleground, at a loss what to do. And as I write about this scenario, I feel the tears in my eyes and a lump in my throat (yes, indeed) at the memory of those terrible mealtime struggles. I can still hear Mum's voice telling me to 'eat a bit more'. And all of this was magnified when we were on holiday, which was the main occasion for eating out. Then the emotional struggle became intensified, but at the same time more difficult to bear, because it was played out in public. Mealtimes in hotels being fixed, whatever I ate was going to be at that time, and of course I couldn't help myself to a snack in the kitchen – I was going to starve (Mum's view, as I imagine now). I was trapped in public with a nagging and unsympathetic mother who made my life misery at mealtimes, so much so that I felt if I ate a mouthful I'd be sick (my view). Mother and daughter were locked together in terrible unhappiness and it's really only now, writing about this, that I recognise just how agonising this was for both of us.

At this point, you probably think you know where this story is going, but, no, it didn't go that way. Remember, this was the 1970s and it really was a different era.

At around the age of thirteen or fourteen, at my all-girls school (the one my mum had attended, to which I was sent at the age of ten), I realised that the Great Bra Race, as I then thought of it, was on, and that I was one of the few without a bra, that essential indicator to teenage girls of growing up and femininity. But, oh dear – I was flat-chested!! My best friend told me that padded bras for teenagers could be bought at British Home Stores (remember them?), so off I went and bought a couple. Just about every other girl in the class wore these bras, I think; they came in particularly lurid colours of magenta (my choice) or turquoise, perfectly calibrated to show through your white school shirt – that may have been the reason for their popularity, of course.

As time went on, my chest never did grow, and I wore my magenta padded bra, which lay flat on my skinny teenage chest, under my school uniform, until one day, in the changing room after a gym session (or games, or swimming, or dance – we had one session of these each schoolday – it was that kind of school), our teacher came in. I caught her taking in my magenta padded bra on my skinny body and giving me a curious glance, and that's when I realised there was no point in wearing it. Casting a glance around the changing room, I noticed properly for the first time how all the other girls in my class, of varying shapes and sizes, filled their bras in a way I didn't. And I realised that it didn't matter.

I must admit that I can't remember now exactly when I stopped wearing a bra, but I did so at some point at school. It dawned on me that it was unnecessary and ridiculous and that I'd be much happier without it. And I was. From that time on, I never bothered about my flat chest, but accepted it.

So, the point of this little anecdote is this: I realised that I could make a virtue out of necessity, love my flat chest and ignore what other people were doing. The need to find clothes that suited me and my shape sparked a lifelong interest in and love of clothes and jewellery, and while it's true that, even today, at the age of sixty-two, I see clothes that I absolutely love, but know I can't wear because of my flat chest, there are lots of other lovely garments I can wear and enjoy wearing. So, I'd say that was a happy situation, wouldn't you?

And the eating thing? As I was saying, that story didn't go the way you may have thought.

I turned thirteen in 1971, and probably if I were that age now, I'd be diagnosed with anorexia. But that wasn't a term in current use at that time. And I'm very thankful that it wasn't, because I was able to grow up and to some extent out of my eating anxiety, naturally and quietly.

Yes, I was skinny, yes, I ate very little, yes, I was an

anxious teenager, but I always knew I was thin. I ate very little, partly because food didn't interest me (and still doesn't, really), partly because of anxiety.

But one benefit that I gained from my mum's constant anxiety about my eating was to learn to ignore, as best I could, her worries about me. I simply zoned them out. And it's a benefit that neither of us could have foreseen, as we sat around the table in our terrible emotional struggle.

Acquiring the habit of zoning out my mum's worries meant that I learned, early on, to pay little or no attention to what anyone else might think or say about me, and not to care about following the herd or bucking expectations.

Leaving behind anxiety was helped by the fact that as I got into my middle teenage years, around fifteen or sixteen, school improved because I could drop sport and maths and physics and chemistry and do the subjects I liked and wanted to sit exams in; Latin, French, Greek, English, history. Bliss! The first time at school and maybe in my life I was able to choose what I wanted to do – and no one could stop me! No wonder I was happier and had less stress in my life.

I'm a quiet, 'respectable' person, but I've never done what I'm told. I won't, you know, march in the streets, write letters to the newspapers, complain about the state of the nation, man the barricades, whatever, because I know that what matters to me is to do exactly what you want, when you want, where you want.

Don't break the law, though. Or be rude.

If you can help it.

Humans are wonderful – intelligent, creative, brave, adventurous, kind, curious, thoughtful – but they're also terrible – coercive, manipulative, wicked, stupid, blinkered, interfering. Don't let anyone else tell you what to do. Ever. You can be a skinny, flat-chested teenage girl who doesn't like food. And there's nothing wrong with you! That's just who you are. Now I'm a skinny, flat-chested woman who doesn't like food and there's nothing wrong with me. That's just who I am.

Don't listen to other people. Don't let them make you believe there's anything wrong with you.

I loved my mum and dad and I know they loved me and meant the best for me. But I know, too, that my mum didn't fully understand me. Dad and I, well, that's another story – we were kindred spirits.

I accepted the way I looked at around fifteen or so and never worried about it afterwards, and I've loved it ever since, because I've loved, really loved, how I look ever since then. Now, at the age of sixty-two, yes, I'm ageing, but I feel the same way about ageing as I do about how I looked at fifteen. I am me and I love me, exactly as I am. I love me, so much. I always will.

So – resist. Whatever the prevailing orthodoxies are, of beauty, appearance, of femininity, of female behaviour, resist them. Stand outside them. Be 'eccentric', 'unconventional'. Find out what you love to do and do it. Once you love yourself as you are you realise it's everyone else who's out of line and you're right. Don't listen to them. Ignore them. Resist.

Resist.

(Actually, I do wear a padded bra nowadays… I feel I can tell you that now we've had this chat).

***

Jane wanted to be a lawyer like her dad, so she went to Edinburgh University and did a law degree, but pretty swiftly, after a year of being a lawyer, decided it wasn't for her. She did a post-grad diploma in Archive Administration and spent the next few decades working as an archivist in Edinburgh. But there was always another pull in her life and nowadays she describes herself as a modern mystic (she runs a Facebook group, The Secret Meditation Garden) and an author. Her first book, Six Enchantments, was published in October 2020. She plans to launch her podcast series, The Secret Spirit, early in 2021.

Refocused Control

Jen Parker

It wasn't primarily about how I looked; for me that was a 'happy' side effect. The reason I started to control what I was eating in the first place was to see if I could. I was in my second year in secondary school, eleven or twelve years old, I'd struggled to make friends and I'd just been rejected from a small friendship circle I thought I'd fit into. They were two girls who'd decided they were better as a duo than a trio. I struggled to understand why they no longer wanted to be my friends, so started to think maybe it was because they were both very slim and very pretty and, perhaps, I was not. I'd always had what my mum called 'puppy fat'. I wasn't overweight, but I had a rounded, chubby face, a pot belly and sturdy legs (helpful for the sports I loved, such as hockey!). She said it would simply fall off as I went through puberty, but I didn't believe her. Perhaps she was right, but I'll never know.

It began with skipping the odd meal. I'd not eat lunch to see if I could make it from breakfast until dinner time without eating. It wasn't every day, at first, but it progressed over the next few months. After a while, I wasn't eating breakfast either, telling my mum that I'd have a 'breakfast bar' on the bus because I didn't have time, but really giving it to my friend sitting next to me. I felt lucky that my friend had a good appetite and was happy to eat my sandwiches too, most days. I'd tell her I'd buy something at school because I didn't want them, and she was baffled because she quite rightly said my mum made the best sandwiches! In reality, I just didn't want to eat anything.

I got a TV in my room at the age of thirteen and was thrilled that I could have a bit more privacy. My mum and my brother were *Star Trek* fans, and I definitely was not, so I'd make the excuse that I'd rather watch something else, and I'd 'eat' my dinner in my room. I would frequently stash it in a carrier bag in my wardrobe, planning to sneak it to the bin when I could get a clear route to it without getting caught. That was an added thrill, avoiding getting caught, but it was mainly for the 'high' of the sense of accomplishment if I could go a whole day without eating.

If I wasn't able to palm off my sandwiches with my friend on the bus, I'd have to sneak them into my homework drawer, again with the intention of getting rid of it when the opportunity arose. Sometimes, however, that opportunity wouldn't arise for a while, and the smell from that drawer and my wardrobe invited questions. I'm pretty sure my mum must have had her suspicions, but I'd just say I must have forgotten an apple from my lunch and escape before any further investigation.

This went on through most of secondary school. Some days I'd have nothing at all to eat, sometimes just a single potato. When I got older, if I couldn't escape having to eat with my family, I'd find new ways to control my calorie intake. I didn't like to put my fingers down my throat, having only tried a few times, so I'd go for a run straight after dinner, pushing myself hard enough to either burn off plenty of the calories, or to be sick. I did have a few questions from friends about my changing appearance. By the time I'd gone into sixth form I had a really good circle of friends and I'd felt settled for a few years. One of my friends openly asked me if I'd lost weight and whether I was okay. I just brushed her off and said I was fine. I would wear baggy clothes to hide my figure and try not to be noticed, but ended up having to pin my trousers with a safety pin to prevent them falling down. I was secretly pleased that my 'puppy fat' was on its way out, and it was a sense of achievement.

But I was tired. So tired. Looking back, I don't know how I still maintained doing sports and achieving good results at school with such a low calorie intake. I do sometimes wonder if I could have achieved more if I hadn't done that to myself, but hindsight isn't very helpful! My moods would be frequently low, I had no energy and I just didn't want to do it anymore. I think I felt less need to do it because I had a stable friendship circle and generally felt better about life. The reasons for controlling my calorie intake (the biggest being the feeling of not being able to control anything else in my life) were decreasing, and I felt like I might need some help.

It was my seventeenth birthday when everything changed. My best friend organised a surprise night out for me, with my mum in cahoots. They arranged for my closest friends to descend on my house for what I thought was a cosy night in, but really she'd arranged for us all to go to a posh restaurant in town followed by a flipping good night out! I know I was underage, but at that time the whole of my year had been going out from the age of fifteen. My best friend wasn't allowed to go out, so she used to stay at my house and then wash her clothes herself when she got home the next day to get rid of the horrendous cigarette smell that used to cling like glue in the days before the smoking ban! My mum said to me, "If I don't let you go out either, you'll both just go to stay at someone else's house, and then you'll have no one to call if you need help. I'd rather trust you to be responsible and know where you are." I respected that, and it did make me more conscious of trying to behave myself on nights out.

However, with hardly eating anything at that age, I'd not be able to handle my alcohol very well. I didn't lose my legs, I'd just be sick fairly early on. But at that age I'd simply be sick then carry on drinking, sometimes being sick several times in a night. I didn't get hangovers, probably a combination of youth and having purged most of the alcohol quickly after consuming. On the night of my seventeenth I had the best night with my friends, dancing the night away, but I was sick quite a bit! Back home, with my friends crammed into my double bed and blow-up beds on the floor, we had a heart to heart. I admitted having issues with my eating. One of my other friends confided that she did too, and we vowed to help each other through it. Thankfully we did, and I was able to gradually increase what I ate until I was eating normally, and by the end of the sixth form I was a lot healthier and felt much better, physically and mentally.

I went away to university, and luckily didn't feel the need to calorie control. I ate a healthy balanced diet, and if I started to gain a couple of pounds through nights out (alcohol and the inevitable end-of-the-night junk food) I'd simply exercise more. I got into jogging and had a dance exercise DVD that I loved, and my weight remained pretty stable the whole way through. I met my now-husband in my fourth year, while I was doing an MSc, and he was in his third year. I'd had a pretty terrible relationship record and was very happily single and much happier in myself, so I was determined to stay that way for my final year. However, I stood on his foot in a club in the first week of the first term, and we instantly hit it off! So much for my single life! Life was good, and I was happy.

When we left university, we had a gap year travelling around the world before starting our intended careers. My best friend and my husband's best friend came with us, as we had been supposed to go with them before meeting each other. It was an amazing experience. I was, however, struggling with carrying my backpack, I had very painful shoulder joints and my back hurt, along with several other joints. I put it down to not having fully recovered from the glandular fever I'd come down with in between university and leaving for travelling, but when my fingers started swelling up, I knew I had to see a doctor. When we landed in Perth, Australia, it was one of the first things I did. A matter of days later I was seeing a rheumatologist on an emergency referral, being told my inflammatory markers were insane and getting diagnosed with a life-changing autoimmune disease. I had ankylosing spondylitis causing inflammation in my spine, pelvis and hips, and psoriatic arthritis causing swelling in my fingers, toes and shoulders, as well as causing psoriasis – mainly concentrated on my scalp.

Although our travelling plans had to change, we still managed to get to all of the countries on our itinerary, although I was gutted we had to miss out going north of Sydney to the Great Barrier Reef. I'll have to go back one day. The changes came because I had to stay in Perth for eight months, instead of the two weeks we'd initially planned. My best friend had already left before the diagnosis because she was doing the last section of our travels in fast forward, but the boys decided to stay with me. Our initial plans had been to spend longer on the east coast, working over there before continuing on to the next countries. However, the recession hit just as we got to Australia, and we heard after we'd all managed to get jobs that it was much harder to do so on the east coast at that time. My mum always said everything happens for a reason, and it does ring true sometimes!

So, we rented a little house, got jobs and I was on the path to getting stable by trialling different medications until one worked well enough for me to continue travelling. Unfortunately, because the drugs took a long time to kick in, the standard process was to be put on steroids to manage the inflammation levels and get the medications to work quicker. My body did not react well to them. I was hungry *all* the time, but the bigger issue was that I'd get *hangry*. If you've not heard that expression, it means that you get angry when you get hungry. I'd feel like I was seeing red, and there were occasions when it actually felt like my blood was boiling for absolutely no reason at all. One method the boys discovered to manage my emotions was carbs. Especially crisps and takeaways. So, for an easy life for all of us, I ate frequently, and I ate a lot. My weight ballooned rapidly and I gained two stone in just a couple of months. When I was able to come off the steroids, I was like a different person! I felt able to exercise again, joined a gym, and we had a much healthier diet, which continued when we then renewed our travels. I wasn't allowed to drink alcohol on my medication, so that helped with the calorie intake! By the time we got home to the UK, I was pretty much back to my normal size.

Over the course of the next few years, with a combination of short-term steroid prescriptions when I was having a flare (when multiple joints swell up, usually caused by an illness or an infection), a stressful job with long hours, and a lack of energy to cook properly, my weight fluctuated a lot. I gradually got bigger, but fooled myself into thinking I wasn't by only wearing stretchy clothes to hide how much weight I'd gained. I'd frequently go on crash diets, cutting out carbs, or only drinking juice for a couple of weeks, and I'd lose a fair bit of weight quickly, but then on it would go, plus some, afterwards. I was in an unhappy cycle of feeling rubbish, so eating rubbish, which would make me feel even more rubbish!

It didn't really hit me just how much weight I'd gained until I fell pregnant with my eldest daughter. I'd had to come off my medication for six months before we were allowed to start trying, then it took four months to conceive, so although I'd been trying to improve my health to prepare for pregnancy, regular bouts of steroids scuppered that! At my first midwife appointment, I was on the borderline between being overweight and being obese (at which point I'd need special extra appointments). They decided to give me the benefit of the doubt and treat me as the top of the overweight spectrum, but I was racked with guilt that I was putting my unborn child's health at risk with my weight. At my first scan, I was terrified that they wouldn't be able to see the baby with the ultrasound through the excess fat. That didn't happen, though!

During the pregnancy I improved my diet and put the baby first. I visibly looked healthier and I felt much better too. I did need extra tests because my ankles kept swelling, I needed a girdle to support my belly because it was straining the muscles supporting it and there was excess fluid in my belly around the baby, but generally it was a healthy pregnancy. When Lily was born, I vowed to improve my health for the good of both of us. I was introduced to Slimming World and it worked perfectly for me. My love of all things carbs didn't have to be punished, as I could eat as much pasta, rice and potatoes as I wanted. It also worked well with the control freak side of my nature as I would write down what I ate, making sure I had enough calcium and fibre, whilst also regulating my 'treats'. Over the course of seven months, I lost four stone and felt amazing when I reached my target.

I felt much happier, but my new weight wasn't without its issues. I never really had any negative comments about my weight when I was overweight. But now I was slim again (I was back to what I perceive as my 'normal' weight, which is the weight I was at university) I had all sorts of negative comments and back-handed compliments. From the comments of, 'You're not going to lose any more weight, are you?' to the standard response of, 'Maybe you should eat more,' if I complained of the cold, they didn't help my self-esteem. I also suffered with loose skin on my belly and my boobs (a combination of having had to have a c-section because of my autoimmune disease, losing weight fairly quickly and breastfeeding) and it made me self-conscious, particularly without clothes on. This made me worry about how much worse it could get if we had the second child that we were planning fairly quickly.

Luckily help was at hand. I reached out to a community of like-minded women on Facebook and voiced my concerns. I was met with a variety of responses, and I really liked looking at the issue from different people's perspectives. I was also lucky enough to work with Ana Bonasera from the Love Thy Body Project on her book, *Stretched*. I provide design and editing services for authors and editing her book gave me a whole new outlook on my post-pregnancy and weight-loss body. Shortly afterwards I worked on a different book project by a body confidence coach, and – combined – their approaches really helped me with my mindset. I stopped talking to myself negatively, I stopped taking other people's negative comments to heart (they were more a reflection on them) and I embraced how I felt about my body.

Because of my hard work getting to my ideal

weight, my second pregnancy was without the guilt, and I enjoyed it even more (I'm lucky to have thoroughly enjoyed both my pregnancies). Not only that, but I knew I was giving my baby a healthier start to her life. It took a little bit longer to lose the weight after my second baby, but I wasn't worried about it. I'd learnt to be kinder to myself. My mum had been diagnosed with cancer for the third time at the start of my second pregnancy and, not long after my baby was born, she rapidly declined. She died when my second daughter was just three months old. I was obviously going through a lot, but rather than turn to comfort eating to cope, I allowed myself to eat 'treats' when I felt like I needed them, without feeling guilty, which would have previously sent me on a downwards spiral of 'to hell with it, I may as well eat everything'. This allowed me to feel my feelings, rather than eating them.

A year later, I was happily maintaining my weight with the 80/20 approach (eating on a healthy plan 80% of the time, and not worrying or feeling guilty about the other 20% of the time). The beginning of December 2019 saw me getting my kit off for a naked calendar, and March 2020 saw me walking the catwalk at an awards ceremony in just lingerie! I still have loose skin on my tummy and boobs, but I feel differently about it. It shows me my hard work getting in shape and breastfeeding my two beautiful girls. I'm not always happy when I look in the mirror, but I am happy a lot more. And when I have those wobbles, I am much better about talking to myself in a better way. I don't want my girls to go through what I did, I want them to love themselves the way they are, and that starts with me loving myself the way I am. I'm not just working on my self-love for me, it's for them too.

***

Jen Parker is thirty-four, mum to two girls, Lily and Amber, aged four and two, and Doug, her eight-year-old pug-shih-tzu cross. She lives in Leicestershire with her husband Aaron. She has worked in the publishing industry for over ten years, and started her multi-award-winning business Fuzzy Flamingo in September 2017, providing editing, design and publishing services to publishing houses and self-publishing authors. She is proud to have designed and edited this book! She is obsessed with flamingos, loves chilling out with a good book and a glass of red and playing with her girls. You can contact her via the following:

www.fuzzyflamingo.co.uk
https://www.facebook.com/FuzzyFlamingoDesign
https://www.instagram.com/fuzzyflamingodesign/
Email: contact@fuzzyflamingo.co.uk

The Little Freckled Pear

Kath Burrows

Once upon a time, many moons ago, in a land far, far away (Hong Kong) a little girl called Kath was born to her English father and Chinese mother. Her mum and dad did the best they knew how with the resources they had at the time. Hong Kong, at that time, was a British Colony and had a diverse and multi-cultural population. For the first few years of her life, Kath lived a happy life and didn't feel any different than anyone else.

By the time she reached primary school age, her parents had decided that it was in her best interests to be sent to an elite girls-only Chinese school, which at the time only seemed to take on Chinese girls. Her dad did not accept this and wrangled his way in so that his daughter would attend this school as the only Eurasian girl in the entire school.

That little girl was me and for the first time in my life, aged about six, I was aware that I somehow looked a bit different to everyone else. I was okay with that as I made some great friends, and no one bullied me for it.

However, it was at about this age that I started getting freckles on my face. As I remember it, this bothered my mum a hell of a lot. I remember wanting to join the Brownies, like so many of my other friends did, but she wouldn't let me because she was afraid that I'd spend too much time outdoors and get even more dark blemishes on my skin.

It was possibly the first time I felt like there was something wrong in the way I looked and that I felt almost like I was not allowed to do something I really wanted as a result of it. For the rest of my primary school years until the age of ten, I recall my mum would do her utmost to make me wear a hat on sunny days and slather me with sunscreen. Hong Kong is sub-tropical, so we did get a lot of sunshine and I enjoyed being outdoors. Despite my mum's best efforts, my face got covered in freckles.

She would lament, 'Oh, it's such a shame that you have freckles, it makes your face look dirty.' As an adult, I now understand that she didn't say this to make me feel ugly and like there was something wrong with me. It was actually her own insecurities and judgements she was projecting onto my younger self. Her feelings were actually well intentioned as she wanted her daughter to be as beautiful as possible and have good prospects. In my experience, like many Asian mums, she believed that being beautiful was of high value to her daughter's prospective future husband. As a young girl she expressed the importance to me of taking care of your looks as a woman to ensure you kept your husband when you were married.

Growing up, I felt that my brother was the good-looking one out of the two of us. He inherited mum's skin, which tanned a beautiful golden brown in the sun, whereas I usually got freckly and sunburnt easily thanks to my dad's genes. Unfortunately for me, my mum's displeasure at my freckles grew even worse when I reached my teens. She would try all manner of 'quack' medicines to try and remove them. I had lotions and potions bought for me to try. I dread to think how harmful some of them may have been now.

At one point she was advised to try using the raw internal organs of a chicken as a remedy to fade those pesky freckles, which simply refused to go away permanently. I cannot accurately describe how nauseating the smell of having that smeared over my face for half an hour regularly was. To try and counteract the awful smell she used to have me sniff a bottle of cheap perfume, which only made it even more vile!

In the end she persuaded me to go to a beautician aged about fifteen to have them frozen off using liquid nitrogen. This whole process probably took about two months and was extremely time-consuming and painful, especially around the sensitive eye area. The freckles would be 'burnt' off by the extreme cold and then blister, scab over and drop off in about a week's time. Once the skin had healed, the procedure would be repeated again and again until they had successfully targeted almost all the freckles I had at the time.

Around the same time as having this done, I was carrying some excess weight and both my brother and dad delighted in tormenting me about it. One time, this chap at my dad's fencing club looked at me and said right in front of me to a group of his friends, 'Hey, look at that white girl, isn't she fat?' He had not realised I fully understood and spoke his language – Cantonese. I felt really ugly, frumpy, full of teenage insecurity. In other words, I felt like I was an embarrassment, a mistake that needed 'fixing'.

One day, my dad and brother were 'teasing' me about my being fat at the family dinner table. I was sobbing and my mum for the first time that I could remember stood up for me and said to my dad: 'David, that's enough!' I felt at least my mum had stood up for me that time.

Over the long summer school holidays that year, I was asked to cat-sit for one of our neighbours. It was the most brilliant paid job I could have as a teen. They asked me to spend as much time as I wanted to keep their cat company and gave me permission to watch their TV and their videos, listen to the radio and do what I wanted whilst I was there.

It was such a blessing; I was in my element. All of a sudden, I had my own private space I could escape to without any of my family interfering and I absolutely adored cats and still do. It was just perfect. It wasn't long until I discovered a Jane Fonda aerobics workout video in their video collection. I was determined to give it a go. The first time I did it, oh my goodness did I huff and puff and thought my head and my heart were going to explode! My face was bright red, and I could barely breathe, but boy it made me feel sooooo good and so proud of myself.

Before I knew it, over the next couple of months, I had lost a whopping 28lbs (2 stone/12.7kg). I also discovered I could control what I ate. I had cut out as much sugar as possible and any foods that I classed as 'bad'. My parents happily bought me a copy of the Jane Fonda video so I could continue to work out at home when my neighbours returned from their holiday. They couldn't believe the transformation in me. I started to spend my pocket money buying tight-fitting clothes to show off my new body. I remember very clearly, I wanted to be 90lbs (41kg), but I was never able to get lower than 92lbs (42kg)

People noticed the huge change and complimented me on the way I looked. I lapped up the compliments and enjoyed how I felt in my new fit and toned body. That was until a sports coach I worked with started to see me in a whole different way. This man had known me from the age of eight, he was my dad's friend and taught me, so I trusted him. He had asked me to assist him when he was teaching kids and paid me for it. I was a very naïve sixteen-year-old, I really didn't get that he was sexually attracted to me. He promised to teach me how to drive in his car and asked me to meet up with him and told me to keep it a secret from my parents.

'How exciting to learn how to drive,' I thought to myself. I turned up where he'd asked us to meet up. He then told me that unfortunately his PA had taken his car and he wasn't sure when she'd be back with it and proceeded to invite me up to his flat. I followed him but soon clocked what his real intentions were; as he pulled my petite body across his I could tell he was sexually aroused. It was in that moment that I knew I had to get out of there. I managed to talk my way out of the situation, made my excuses and walked back home as fast as I could. Thank goodness nothing more happened but it shook me up.

I told my parents what had happened straight away, I was frightened and crying about it. My mum blamed me, telling me how stupid I was, and my dad told me that as my sports coach was such a large, muscular man, he couldn't really challenge him. My dad also expected me to continue working for him as he had arranged for him to be one of my referees for my university application. You can imagine how that felt.

It was probably around then that I became interested in being physically strong as a way of protecting myself as much as I was able. I would go to the gym every day and lift as heavy weights as I could, I would run and do my Jane Fonda video because it was something I could control. However, no matter what I did I still had this horrid pervasive thought of being 'not good enough'.

It was 1993, I had moved from Hong Kong to the UK to study at uni. I was lucky enough to meet my soulmate there within a few weeks and before long we were engaged. My fiancé then and now husband delights in cooking for others. It's one of his ways of expressing love. I was in love with him, the first and only serious relationship I've ever had. For the first time in a few years, I relaxed a bit and didn't exercise so much and ate whatever my wonderful man cooked up for me. By the end of our first term at uni I had put on 10lbs.

I flew back to Hong Kong over the Christmas period to be with my family. One morning I was out for a little jog when again a young Chinese man piped up to his friends, 'Hey, look at that white girl jogging, doesn't her bum look big?' One of his lady friends told him that he was not being very kind but that didn't make me feel any better about myself. None of them had realised I could understand them perfectly well.

After this I became much stricter about what I ate and made sure I exercised even more. Alas, I was blessed or cursed (depending on how you look at it) with a curvy bum. It didn't matter how much I exercised, that was always a part of me that resisted getting smaller. What made it even more noticeable was that in my mind I looked disproportionate. I had this tiny waist and what I thought was a massive behind and big thighs, so I was a petite but curvy pear.

There were many years after that I spent religiously reading food labels, making sure that they didn't contain any more than 5% sugar, checking the fat content and at the height of it I'd be going to the gym three times a day – once before work, once at lunchtime and then after work. Even if I was ill, I'd still make myself go to the gym as I'd mentally beat myself up if I didn't. My self-worth was tied up with how much I exercised and only eating 'good' foods. I would attach either guilt or shame if I didn't exercise or eat 'clean'. I was a perfectionist and wanted to be as perfect as possible in every way I could.

It was years later when I was offered a ten-week mindfulness course on the NHS following a bout of depression that I started becoming curious about how the mind works. I also somehow unwittingly fell into yoga. At first it was much more about the physical aspects of yoga but as I became more and more aware of the philosophy behind it, it started to open the door for my own self-discovery and self-compassion. This, in turn, allowed me to understand other people's behaviours better and I was able to forgive how I had treated myself.

In 2015 I started my yoga teacher training, something to this day I will always be very grateful for. When I started it, I had been suffering with depression and I didn't even know if I wanted to teach it. At my lowest I didn't even have the energy to load the washing machine and absolutely loathed myself.

At the time I did it for myself to help me heal myself. Luckily, I was also seeing a brilliant yoga therapist and within three months I felt much more like myself again. She taught me breathing techniques and would create poses that challenged me, so I had no choice but to stay focused in the present moment. This meant that I could at least momentarily be freed from the tyranny of my mind.

At the same time, I started to post a daily 'gratitude with attitude' post on my Facebook page and ended up doing this for three years. Over the past four years I've invested time and money in myself and my well-being and also qualified as a holistic mindset coach. The mindset work really helped me deal with my inner critic, so I could stop being so critical of myself.

All of these things have helped me change my relationship with myself enormously in a positive way. It has the added bonus of improving my relationship and understanding of other people too and having empathy with their struggles and self-sabotaging behaviours.

Fortunately, I've been free from depression for several years now and can honestly say that I am much more relaxed about what I eat and no longer feel bad if I take a break from working out.

It took me years to get this far but I don't want others to suffer that long, so in 2020, I set up my

Facebook community 'The Body Love Lounge' to create a safe space to help women become confident and compassionate about their bodies so they can start to show up unapologetically in all areas of their life to create the happiness they want.

***

Kath's experiences sparked a life-long passion to focus on both physical and mental health and wellness and led her to qualifying as a personal trainer, fitness instructor, yoga teacher and most recently as an AcroYoga teacher and mindset coach.

Having experienced depression in her adult life, she found that regular yoga and meditation combined with working on her mindset have successfully kept it at bay. She realised the power of training the mind regularly as well as the body and understood the mind-body connection. This led to her developing herself as a holistic mindset coach. She specialises in helping women become confident and compassionate about their bodies by transforming their inner critic into their inner cheerleader, so that they are empowered to show up unapologetically in all the areas of their life to create the happiness and success they want.

Kath is passionate in her belief that the combination of physical and mental practices can be the catalyst to help others explore their true potential by overcoming their self-sabotaging thoughts, behaviours, fears and limitations in a safe and supportive space.

FB group:
https://Facebook.com/groups/thebodylovelounge

FB business page:
@bodylovealchemist

IG account:
@bodylovealchemist

Courage

Nicola Reynolds

Addiction – defined as an urge that you cannot control, something you either desire, crave or cannot function without. In my case this addiction is something we cannot live without. Food, our essential sustenance, a necessity for feeding our body nutrients and energy. The bane of my life and a roller coaster driven by emotions, manipulation and health issues.

I've had a love-hate relationship with food all my life. I grew up with a limited palate. I was an extremely fussy eater. But I was energetic and exercised a lot. It wasn't until I was at university that the weight started to pile on. Nights out, takeaways, comfort food – sugar cravings to get through long hours of study.

I joined weight loss programmes, learned to cook and eat the fruits and vegetables I'd never eaten before and extended my palate to levels I'd never imagined, but my habits always reverted back. The weight just kept creeping on slowly. By the time I married in 2005, I was about fourteen stone. It was out of my comfort zone, but I lived with it. My life felt like a diet. All the women in my family are large, I never really considered it a bad thing, but I really didn't like what I saw in the mirror.

I would starve and punish myself, then find myself needing a burst of carbs to recover. It wasn't a good thing to do. It was only skipping the odd meal, but my body really didn't cope well. In 2008 when we started trying for a baby, I was diagnosed with an underactive thyroid, which explained some of the weight gain and how my body reacted to certain behaviours. It did create difficulties with my cycles trying for a baby. I was referred to a specialist. I found out I was pregnant the day before the appointment. I attended anyway as my cycle had been three months long at that point, and I was unsure how many weeks pregnant I was. I was given a smear, a full panel of blood works and told that I shouldn't be too confident about the pregnancy. He was born nine months to the day by my reckoning, not the hospital's who dated him as premature. When I arrived at the hospital in labour with my TENS machine going, the nurses tried to convince me I only had a urine infection. He was born a few hours later.

Almost three years later, my daughter brought with her the most catalysts for change, through no fault of her own. Her arrival was by emergency caesarean, I haemorrhaged, lost a lot of blood, had issues with the rhesus factor (I'm rhesus negative – she's positive), and the healing following the birth led to extreme weight loss.

The trauma from the birth had triggered an

autoimmune response in my body. My underactive thyroid had flipped its switch to become an overactive thyroid. I was diagnosed with Graves' disease. I lost four stone in a short space of time but my body had all manner of other more frightening symptoms. I was having heart palpitations, panic attacks and it was scary. Once treatment for the Graves' disease started, the weight piled back on and the fatigue set in.

I was now looking after two children as a full-time stay-at-home mum. My husband had insisted I gave up my career and stayed home rather than pay out for childcare. I was losing Me! Sleepless nights, night feeds, no ability to share that burden as I was breastfeeding and by the time my daughter was fourteen months old, I hadn't had a full night's sleep for over three years. I was like a well-tuned routine machine. I functioned for the use of others. Days would pass before I'd remember to shower or bathe. In the list of priorities, I was at the bottom. Even below the cats.

I blamed myself, my weight, that I didn't do enough, that I wasn't a good wife. But in retrospect, I was the one putting my all into everything we had. I cared for everyone but myself. When my husband left, I had no idea who I was, I felt like an empty shell – complete nothingness!

My identity was mum, daughter and wife – but who was I?

I looked back and realised I'd spent nearly all my life trying to fit into someone else's box, fulfil someone else's needs and lived and fulfilled the dreams of others, other than my academic journey, which was partly to prove to my brother and cousins that we really can do what we want with our lives. I realised I'd lived to serve others far too much.

My friendship circle dissolved quickly, our shared friends just didn't know what to say to me and it was easier for them to associate themselves with my ex-husband as the kids were with me full time.

Which left me empty, lonely, without an identity and lacking any direction.

I fell into deep depression. One of the hardest things I ever had to accept was going to the doctor and admitting how low I was. I went for counselling. I learned to accept help. But food was still a huge issue to me. I couldn't stomach food in my deepest darkest days, and I was prescribed Complan shakes so I could take my medications safely.

In an attempt to fix my poor relationship with food, I tried all manner of eating plans and even hypnosis to enable me to lose weight. But none have worked for long enough to have a lasting impact.

It was two years before I felt brave enough to start dating again. My children were aged three and six at the time. I was feeling at the height of my prime. I had found my confidence, found me and loved what I was doing. I had my own little bakery company selling bread and cake at craft fairs. It was hard work, but it helped me find a purpose again.

I met a nice older guy, and fell for him hard and fast. We were inseparable. We struggled to be apart from each other. He recognised my Asperger's syndrome in me. I approached my GP about being assessed and got diagnosed at thirty-seven. It gave me a lot of answers to how and why I have certain ways of thinking and behaviours.

But I was still vulnerable and was struggling with the divorce from my children's dad. My new partner was trying to help but his opinions were strong and sometimes threatening. He often suggested that I should give up custody to prove a point, but I never wavered in my commitment to my children. They are my world!

My life was once again plagued by health issues, the stresses of the divorce and demands from my new partner left me constantly exhausted and I started to get headaches. I went for an eye test, which resulted in a trip to A&E. I had excess fluid on my brain. I had to have a lumbar puncture to drain away the excess. It left me very ill the following days. I ran the risk of needing a brain stent to get it under control. I feared this would have other implications, so I worked on getting well.

During this time, I closed my bakery business and opened my web solutions business. It enabled me to still have a hands-on business but without the early mornings and late nights needed to produce my products that had a very short shelf life.

Six months later, when the headaches started again, I was admitted for another lumbar puncture. This one left me with Bell's palsy on the left side of my face, which is a facial stroke; I could no longer smile.

By that time my partner and I were due to get married in the June. My children were five and eight by this point and I was determined to have my smile back in time for the wedding. It was a small wedding, but not without its issues. As the bride I should have been enjoying the day but instead I was left running about topping up the buffet and serving drinks. I barely got a chance to talk to the guests and my new husband was in the most foul mood possible.

He even left me at the hall and went home for a sleep. Leaving me between the afternoon and evening parts of the wedding stranded at the hall without a car, pretty much alone.

I was distraught, it didn't feel like a partnership at all. What had I married into? I felt like a possession!

After the wedding, he was more controlling. He'd fully moved into my house, we were living as a family, and he barely lifted a finger to help. Again, I lost myself. Over the two years we were together he managed to erase any essence of the me I'd discovered. My self-worth was at an all-time low.

The get out clause came two months after marriage. Two police officers woke me one morning, and my new husband was arrested for looking at indecent images of children. My world shattered. I almost lost my children; social services had encouraged the children's dad to start custody proceedings. At first, I thought the pictures could have possibly been those close to adult teens, but they weren't, they were children as young as eight.

Trying to break free from him was the hardest thing I've ever had to do. Both being Christian, I was struggling with abandoning my vows a second time. He had brainwashed my head into believing all manner of stuff, he broke me in so many ways. Ways I never thought possible. I felt spiritually broken – at odds with my faith. I felt ashamed, and like I'd failed to protect my children.

Social services were crawling all over me like ants, judging my parenting and me! I felt naked! However, after a few assessments on the children they determined they hadn't been touched by him. I changed my name by deed poll and approached a solicitor for a divorce!

Then I hit a brick wall! I had to wait until the following year to start the divorce proceedings. I found my kin within Women's Aid, they helped me understand what I'd been through. I started to realise it wasn't all my fault. Things that happened were beyond my control. My counselling started, I rebranded my business, and totally locked the ex out of my life.

That had repercussions – harassment, demands, letters – and ignoring it was hard, but it was needed to enable me to move on.

It left me in a delicate state of anxiety for a

considerable length of time. I found myself ill again. My body took over, started to fight against me. After a two-week hospital stay, I was diagnosed with a rare autoimmune condition called Churg Strauss. My blood was attacking my body, affecting my organs. It made my asthma worse, I could hardly breathe.

My weight has always been a topic of conversation with my GP and my consultants. Just eat salad they would say – as someone who had a limited palate it's hard to just eat salad. My weight is stubborn as I'm now dependant on steroids to stop my blood destroying my organs. The prognosis on my condition is poor if left untreated – I now take weekly tablets of chemo as well.

Each knock back took part of me with it. I turned to counselling and self-development to find myself. I decided that no matter how hard it was for me to lose weight due to my medications I would learn to love the skin I was in!

It hasn't been an easy journey; my first task was to erase the vicious voice of my ex from inside my head. He was the initiator in my web business, but he never held any stake in it. It was mine – but this horrid niggle was there in my head. That horrid voice that told me I was useless without him when I tried to work. It was the most amazing feeling the day I realised it had finally silenced – it was also around the time when I started walking tall and noticed how beautiful the world was again. Up to that point it hadn't occurred to me I'd spent so much time looking down at the floor.

My strength was coming back to me, I was healing and starting to attract new business and friendships. It was strange that most of the businesses I was attracting were from the same industry – holistic and spiritual healing. It was here that a key part of me started to heal. I still had a huge gaping hole where my faith was. I was desperate to heal that void but venturing into a church reduced me to a quivering wreck every time. I made use of the faith centre whenever I was at the hospital, but the spiritual healing was calling out to me. I learned to meditate, I learned to read oracle cards, I reached out to my spiritual calling and in doing so began to embrace the authentic me.

The wholeness I was feeling had a domino effect on the other areas of me. My prices for my business began to creep up as I began to recognise my self-worth, and my confidence increased. I felt able to talk openly about my story and got it printed in a book. I met an amazing group of women in the process, who I consider my soul sisters. The journey we took together was one I will never forget.

On returning from the book writing retreat I was awarded with the divorce certificate – it was all finally over! I recently celebrated my one-year divorceversary – yes it is a thing! Anyone who's left a controlling or abusive relationship would celebrate any milestone of cutting contact from such creatures.

I am still pursuing my spiritual healing and

meditate regularly. It allows me to reflect on just how far I have come. Life has presented me with many struggles, and I won't claim to have improved my addictive relationship with food, but I have certainly improved my relationship with myself.

I no longer give myself a hard time about having a bad day. My inner voice is much kinder these days. I perform my duties as a single mum to the best I can be on any given day. The children know I have low energy days due to my conditions. It doesn't make them love me any less, because I know to them I am their world – and I know I wholeheartedly give them everything they actually NEED, regardless of whether they have a WANT I cannot provide. One thing that will always stay with me is my eldest turning to me at the launch of the last book and telling me how proud he was of me. It still makes me cry now when I think about it. I can't think of anything more precious to hear when my children have seen me go through a lot to hear those words – I'm proud of you mummy!

I don't mean to sound self-righteous when I say that a lot of what I did I did purely for me and my healing. To allow me to come out of all this on the other side as a functional person. But there is still a lot of love, happiness, kindness and courage sitting in me right here as I'm typing the last paragraph of my story. I won't profess to have all the answers, and there were very dark moments as well, but knowing what I have accomplished and where I am now, I can repeat these words back to myself with confidence: I'm proud of who I am!!

***

Nicola Reynolds is a single mum of two. She owns a web solutions business in Nottinghamshire called Pixie-Box.co.uk, is co-author of *Rise of the Mumpreneur* and she has overcome many health and relationship issues. She loves meditating and reading oracle cards in her spare time to the lovely ladies in the divine femine group. She has also been a huge supporter of Love Thy Body Project since the start, and has taken part in many of the workshops and courses to assist with her self-love journey. She also enjoys gaming with her children and curling up on the couch with her small dog with a good film or book.

If you want to connect With Nicola, her business Facebook is www.facebook.com/mspixiebox or website is pixiebox.co.uk

She celebrated her fourth year in business by taking the leap into a limited business status.

Make the Path Your Own

Sally Anne Saint

I came from a home where self-love and respect for being a woman was so so low.

In healing my own path back to the place of self-worth, self-love and self-respect, I bear witness to the transformative path you step on.

Everything changes, everything.

In coming home to this place, I heal the family line and live an authentic life.

I wrote these words months ago when I applied to be part of this collaborative project, and here they are as I write; they are the anchor for my writing, the heart of a woman resides in these words, a heart that feels and expands, thanks to the journey of self-love.

Last night I had a dream, and it was not one of those fluffy and fun ones, it was a deeply intense one. I had this energy penetrate me and it was about to go for my son. I woke to stop it, actually woke and I even put on my glasses, which are stored next to my bed. I checked around and was on red alert. I then went back to sleep but the memory of this attack through me that was going to my son was in my mind.

When I woke, I saw a clear message that I must transform my past so it doesn't pass on to my son. I woke and stopped it, so I wake up now. I wake up to the responsibility of being a guide to my son, and that what I carry must stop with me.

And this is where my story takes you, dear reader, the journey of being the full stop. I am that full stop for my family. It takes one, just one to break a family line and it sets all others free, past, present and future are affected by the work I have done. Was it easy? Hell no.

My full stop came with so much pain, but also it was worth it; a moment where I lost everything actually meant it set me free, for it takes the final straw, that last push that feels like it will break you, to make you stop. To make you say enough, to make you stand up and say 'no'.

This is the way, so whether it is ill health, a terrible situation, that challenge that makes you take your breath in sharply and not able to exhale so easily, then this is your place, your place and space of transformation.

It takes the final one, the curtain comes down on the way you have lived your life and it can only rise again when the commitment to change has been acknowledged. I am here to bear witness to this moment, to connect you and myself to the importance of the breaker and maker. The one that comes into your homes like Thor's hammer, the blow of which can be felt from miles away and there is no way you can get back up after that knock.

I hold space for every woman who has felt this cataclysmic blow. For the months that follow afterwards where nothing you did before works, what came before doesn't matter and for a time it just feels like survival. The betrayal of a loved one, the assault, the violent act, the scam, the health scare. That which will not lie down and be. Here is the moment, here is the life-changer, here is the door opener to self-love.

For here there is no other way, nothing else will work, there is nowhere else to go. Here self-love walks with you, whispering in your ear that this is the way. This is the ONLY way dear woman, the only way. If you are here, breathe in these words if you are struggling, if you feel lost, if you feel broken, if you feel you cannot keep going. Know this is the way, and what feels like the end is actually the beginning.

Your old way of being has to end, your old way of seeing yourself is slowly killing you, day by day, you are being suffocated. You didn't know you were, for it has become a way of being, it was so subtle that it has felt like normal, the way you have treated yourself has been your personal barometer for how others appeared in your life and it had to change.

It had to change with the awfulness of that person, that pain, that hurt, that betrayal, that health scare. It had to. Know that here lies your personal medicine, right here, know that as you feel the ending, the loss, the pure undeniable pain, there is an opening. Know it is here, right here, where you need to be.

I will now go to my beginning where I grew up on a family farm, with parents who loved me but whose deeply traumatic childhoods meant they were unable to hold a safe home; extreme people were part of my growing up. Extreme men and women.

My idea of normal behaviour from others was so off-balance that I attracted and let in the most unhealthy people. Over the years I was bullied at school, felt unsafe at home, I have been abused, hit, controlled and this was for a massive part of my life.

Yet the missing ingredient in all these above is self-love. If you look at a baby and young child, you see the love they have for themselves when they look in the mirror. They are fascinated by what they see, they have no separation from this natural state of being.

Fear puts us all in a different state, a separation of self. As a child, we are dependent on our caregivers to create and hold a safe environment and if that is missing then the child has nowhere to go, so they separate. I separated, I hid away, even from myself, my greatest gifts. There was nowhere to put them.

I remember one key moment in my childhood, I was at school, the school where I was bullied by a gang of girls, the leader of which was called Sarah. I distinctly recall wanting to change my name to hers as I viewed her life to be the one of power and mine as none.

In the school there was lots of outdoor space, it was a small village one with idyllic fields to play in, cherry trees that would give the most remarkable blossom every single year. Kind dinner ladies and some kind teachers but also too much space and not a strong structure around supervision of that space, Now, as an adult, I can see the impossible task of trying to keep eyes on the children in such a vast setting.

The memory that springs to mind was of me sitting outside on the steps of a classroom, with a friend. We were sitting side by side and chatting about things now I can no longer recall but we were happy. She was a sweet girl and we naturally got on, but she was the younger sister of one of the girls in the gang of bullies.

As we sat chatting the gang came along and saw us together. The older sister told the younger sibling off for being with me, they then grabbed her and tried to pull her away. We clung together, arms linked, trying to stay together, but we had no power against the gang.

She was pulled away and I was left alone, on a cold concrete step with no one, and my crime? I honestly don't know what it was, was it that I breathed? Was it that I actually had a friend that annoyed these girls so much? That someone chose to be with me, without control or manipulation?

Now as I write this, at the age of forty-eight, I have tears running down my cheeks, for the little girl sitting on the step, the little girl not allowed to have friends, or joy in her life, unless the gang said so. How truly heartbreaking that as a child of about seven or eight I desperately wanted to change my name to my persecutor's.

You see the bullying started when I was very young and continued through the whole of my primary school years. Not a teacher or member of staff saw and my family were in too much of a state to see my pain, the pain in a young child's eyes, with nowhere to go and no choices of her own.

My days were controlled by others, all my days. At home there was a live-in alcoholic workman, who ruled my mother completely. A father who was unable to speak up. Extreme people stepped in and out of my childhood, and became the norm, and not one of them saw me.

It was only when I left for secondary school that the bullying stopped for me. I found out much later that the bullies continued to bully, but it was no longer me on their radar. Yet the compounded control and loss of identity has been something I have worked with all my adult life.

I now see with compassionate eyes how I was stripped of humanness by the bullies, how alone I was, so desperately alone. In a way, I stayed the little girl on the concrete step with no one and too afraid to reach for any joy in case it was taken away from me. For it is better to ask for nothing than to try and it is ripped from you by others, others who neither care nor see you. Whose only mission is to deny you any rights at all.

This is one moment in my history, one, there are countless, hundreds of moments, moments where what I had was taken, my self-worth and self-love were the invisible pieces stolen from me. Eroded by repetition and no one seeing, for it would have taken just one adult, just one.

Self-compassion and new understanding flow through me as I visit this place and space. I see my own path, but I also see my mother's, my auntie's, my grandmother's, my sister's, my ancestors crowd around me, for I have just given words to their pain also.

I have opened the door to their suffering, their path, and in doing so may I lay to rest their aching hearts also, for all they would have wanted was exactly the same thing, for one adult to see. One adult to act on their behalf, one. So, I am now that adult. May I now reset history for us all. In all time and space, as we are connected, may this be the peace for us all.

As I write these words I have YouTube playing on my laptop also and it has just moved automatically to an 'enhance self-love music' piece. How magical is this?

You see, self-love means exactly what it says, SELF-love, to give oneself that which is needed, to see the pain and hold space for it. To allow ourselves to remember and, with soft eyes and a loving heart, surround our younger selves with the gentlest glow of love.

As I sit here there is so much compassion and love flowing for that little girl on the steps. All she went through, she is a wonder, she has shown such strength and courage, for it was her who got up every day, who went on the school bus and got through every day, on her own. The gang needed the numbers, she had no choice but to stand alone, and she did.

The girl on the steps created the most amazing artwork, so amazing her headteacher thought she had cheated in a class competition, she hadn't, the teacher never gave her the chance to speak, but the girl knew the truth.

The girl on the steps developed such a bond with animals and nature that she could feel the energy of the buzzing bees in the cornfield, she could sense the heart of every animal around her and they knew hers.

The girl on the steps would take in injured animals, the majority of which would die, but she gave her best, she loved them, she cherished her time with them, and she buried them in the garden with the help of her dear mother.

This young girl found her way through the harshest of environments, this girl chose to love, at first with animals, which were her safe zone. Somehow with each beating of the heart drum in each creature, it kept the rhythm of her heart going enough, gave her the energy and the space to do one thrum then another. From one animal to another, the baton passed, the thrum of the girl's heart kept going.

Until she was ready, until the universe gave her enough space, enough tools, enough tears, enough energy, enough.

Now here I stand, the woman, the woman who loves, the woman with scars, the woman with a history she has worked with, remembered and learnt to love.

You see the journey of self-love is a lifetime's practice, a practice which is key to you having enough energy, enough yes's inside and enough no's. It's the key to living a life that is technicolour rather than black and white.

It is key to living, key. So, as you step into your days, create space for things that nourish you, things that inspire you, people who truly love you and see you. Cut out the drains on your energy, harsh people, negative situations, just cut it out.

Give yourself and your family the brightest beacon to be around and to light their paths, for when we relearn to love ourselves, we become the most beautiful sight for those around us. With self-love, we change our lives, our homes. Our circumstances and the world we live in.

I set my family free from the bonds of invisibility, of denying joy for fear of others taking it from them. I free my energy to keep expanding and growing, I free my career path so it can grow and carry me on its sacred way. I free my heart to love, love deeply, more deeply because of the pain transformed.

I love me. Want to join me? Look back with

compassion at where you have been, allow the tears, allow the memories, surround yourself with loving arms as you do so, your arms, yours.

Now the path is open to you, step onto it.

Much love.

***

Sally Anne Saint is the founder of Wise Woman Guide. She is dedicated to empowering women with everything that she does. To connect with her go to her website: www.wisewomanguide.co.uk.

Being Different

Sarah Reaves-Town

It's taken me forty-six years to be okay with being different. I'll say that again… forty-six years.

How am I different? Well, it's more of a feeling rather than anything particularly visual. Some of you will know what I'm talking about, that feeling of not quite belonging, not quite fitting in.

I guess it started way back in my childhood with my first school experience. I was accepted into a convent school in a small Leicestershire village. I wasn't Catholic… I was from a broken home. That's obviously not so unusual now but at the time and in that wealthy sleepy village it was pretty huge. I used to think that I felt different because of being from a single parent family, living with my grandparents, but looking back I'm not sure it was that, I just didn't feel like I shared any similarities with the other children.

As it turned out, I didn't have long to experience the joys of the convent school. My mum remarried when I was six years old, which meant changing schools and, worst of all, leaving the safety and security of my grandparents, who I considered to be like my parents. It was a deeply confusing time and I felt very scared. It was only a matter of months until my first half-sibling came along; this is when the feelings of disconnection started to take root. My wonderful grandparents suggested I go and live with them for six weeks after the birth of my half-brother so that my mum could spend some time with her new family. It was an offer made with kindness and I loved to be with my grandparents but for me this led to a deeper sense of not being wanted by my mum and new family. It also meant that I needed to change schools again for just six weeks.

Fast forward a few years and two further half-siblings, I was spending pretty much every weekend with my grandparents. I wanted space and hated being at home. For me it was a constant reminder of how I wasn't needed and how they had a better time without me... was this really how it was? Probably not but, when you are eleven, it's hard not to take things to heart. At my grandparents', I got the attention I so badly craved. It was very easy for me to make the connection between how I was feeling and the situation with my family. Did I blame them? Absolutely. Was it really their fault that I was feeling unwanted? Definitely not. It took me a very long time to make the realisation that my mum was just doing the best that she could whilst raising a large family that included one particularly difficult eleven-year-old.

My memories of my primary school years were a bit of a blur. I have literally blanked them from my memory bank. I'm serious, when I get to reminiscing with my longest friend from school it's like we went to completely different schools! I can't remember anything! Okay, so that's not strictly true, I remember some stuff...

The time I was asked to sing the scales during a music lesson and despite my pleas of having a sore throat, the teacher insisted. The sound that came out of my mouth was broken and comical, so of course the whole class laughed... they laughed and so did the teacher.

The time I was paired up for country dancing with the tiniest boy in the class and my teacher casually said in front of the class, "Now Sarah, be careful you don't catapult Paul into the air when you swing him around." The class laughed... so did the teacher.

The time the whole class had to weigh ourselves for a maths lesson and the teacher wrote all of our weights on the blackboard and went on to put them in order of heaviest to lightest... you've guessed it, I was the heaviest and took pride of place at the top of the board.

I hated those years of school so much. I didn't feel like I belonged there. I convinced myself that it was all a big mistake and that there was a different school I should be at... like a boarding school out of an Enid Blyton book or, better still, the school of Mildred Hubble from *The Worst Witch*. Then the lies started. I used to tell everyone that I was a witch and that I could cast spells. I stayed in character all day, sometimes never realising that unconsciously I was becoming a self-fulfilling prophecy… I was making myself different. This continued throughout my school career. I became the class clown, making everyone laugh. I became the rebel, being dared to do things, making bad choices in the desperate attempt to fit in and be accepted. Was I ever not accepted? I'm not sure. All I know is that during all my different roles I had no idea who I was.

I feel like my whole teenage life and into my early adulthood was dominated by scrutinising my appearance. I was too fat, my nose was too big, one eye was bigger than the other, my legs were too short, my body was too long, my boobs were too big, and I had, what we now call, a resting bitch face. I was the first in my school year to wear a bra, I was the first to start my periods.

I began to hate how I looked, and I was determined to change it because, surely, this was the reason that I didn't fit in. The key to being accepted was to change how I looked.

So, what did I do?

Well, for a good few months, I slept with a peg on my nose to try to make it look thinner… yes, I really did do that.

I went on a diet of my own making, which involved skipping meals and doing a lot of exercise in my bedroom.

I experimented with what is now called contouring, using different shades of eyeshadow on my face to change the appearance of my features.

And, you know what? It worked. Well, not the peg thing, that was never going to be a success, was it? But I lost weight, my body changed, and I appeared to look different, but what I was shocked to realise was that the physical transformation didn't change how I felt inside. I still felt different. I was devastated. I was still the same fat old Sarah on the inside, not feeling accepted. I had put all my hopes into this, losing weight and changing my appearance was supposed to change everything for me. I felt bereft and lost. I didn't know where else to go. I came to the realisation that I clearly hadn't done enough. I needed to be more extreme, so in desperation I stopped looking in the mirror, and I began this strange habit of not being able to name or acknowledge some of my body parts. I actually couldn't bring myself to say the words "toes" and "feet".

All of a sudden, I became very aware of my sexuality and I absolutely hated it. To me the feet seemed very provocative and intimate, so I completely banned the very idea of them from my consciousness. To this day I have never come across anyone else who has experienced such a thing, so, if you are reading this and have had a similar experience, I'd love to hear from you.

I made bad choices, which brought about

experiences that would change my life in so many ways that continue to haunt my memory, but these are not to share or delve into now. What is important to note here is that life is rich with experience… there are no good or bad experiences but simply experiences. It's how we choose to react to them that defines them to be good or bad. Do we learn from them and change our path, or do we strap the weight of guilt to our hearts in the hope that we won't make the same mistake again? Now, if this is an unfamiliar concept to you, may I suggest that you note it down now, it may just change your life.

I left home when I was nineteen years old to buy my first house with my then boyfriend who would shortly become my first husband and, much later, father to my eldest daughter. This was a wonderful time of independence for me and whilst that brought a lightness to my being, I was still struggling to identify who I was. It seemed everyone around me was defined. They knew what they wanted to do with their life, they had a style, knew who they were and what they stood for. Was that ever really true? Probably not but the grass is always greener on the other side, isn't it?

So, when did all of this change for me? Well, I'd love to say that there was an epiphany moment when I began my journey into independence and adulthood, but you already know that's not true. I continued to stagger blindly through the forest of my life and experiences. Now, this all seems like a pretty bleak existence but of course it wasn't like this always. The independence and freedom I got from adulthood was studded with wonderful times and experiences, but I continued to avoid mirrors. I took on a new habit of self-criticism, which consisted of me naming everything I hated about myself. I did it pretty much every day, memorising the list of flaws and faults in my physical being. I kept a written list of everything I would change about my body when I had the money for plastic surgery. Underneath all the beautiful life experiences I was still sad, desperate Sarah... lost in the twists and turns of life.

For the purpose of keeping my story brief and to the point, I'm going to fast forward a few years. This is not to say that the events that passed are not noteworthy, merely deserving of a whole other story. So, we pass dramatic, yet stunning scenery of a house move, job change, miscarriage, birth of my eldest daughter and sadly but not surprisingly divorce.

What I should mention here is that in and amongst my attempt at self-discovery I found yoga. Now, you may think this an obvious turn in the tale and maybe it is, but it wasn't all rainbows and unicorns from the first downward facing dog, I can tell you. In all honestly, I can say that I dabbled with yoga, it was a physical practice for me and nothing more... at the beginning. I practiced yoga on and off for ten years before I actually plucked up the courage to walk into a real-life yoga class. I did all of my practice via the miracle of DVD and then later online.

Divorce was a desperate time for me but also a time of transformation. I continued with the physical practice of yoga here and there but the thing that was the pivotal embryo of change for me was journaling.

Once it became clear that there were no amounts of flat screen TVs, gadgets and gismos that would save my first marriage I started to look at the prospect that lay before me. Separation, moving home with my parents, being a single mum, sharing custody and I realised that it was going to be a huge and rugged journey that I couldn't face alone. I needed a friend that I could trust and confide in, I needed someone who wasn't afraid to challenge me and to tell me when I was wrong. Someone I could confess my deepest and darkest thoughts and emotions to. It was a shock to say the least when it dawned on me that there was nobody I was prepared to share all of that with... nobody that is except me. So, I turned to journaling all of my thoughts, emotions and wild ramblings into a notebook every single evening without fail. It was a raw and deeply honest account of what I was experiencing and an absolutely no holds barred vulnerability. On these sheets of paper, I could finally be fully and unapologetically me.

Journaling absolutely helped me to get through the rough and tumble of my journey through separation and divorce. Did journaling help me to accept who I was and to start to look with a kindly, soft gaze into the mirror? No, not at first. It just helped me to see where the gaps were, to understand and unravel old experiences and how they affected my reactions to emotions that surfaced.

Over time I began to connect yoga and journaling with self-care. These were both practices where I could dedicate fully to myself for a small amount of time every day. This became an immeasurably beneficial ritual, which in time would lead me along a very unexpected path.

The years continued to be scattered with life changes: college, university, a second marriage and a second child. Again, as before, the details of these times are deeply important to my story but are worthy of more word and description than I can afford here.

The unexpected adventure I would take came to me one day as I scrolled through social media and found a post advertising yoga teacher training local to where I lived. Up until that very moment in time I had never considered teaching yoga as a profession. Why? Because I didn't look like a yoga teacher. I wasn't tall and willowy. I was a short and stubby middle-aged woman who drank too much and didn't look after herself very well. I realise now, of course, that was a wildly judgemental mindset to have, but at the time it was real for me. I have no idea to this day what made me sign up for the twelve-month course, but I can honestly say it has changed my life. I'm not suggesting for a moment that we all need to become yoga teachers to be better connected with ourselves, but I am suggesting that we should all practise yoga.

My training took me on a journey of self-discovery.

I learnt to regard yoga as not just a physical practice as I had done before, but more of a philosophy for life. I didn't realise at the time but, through journaling, I had started to reconfigure my mind to find clarity and yoga helped me to accept the limitations of my body. To feel okay with where I was physically, what I looked like and what my body was capable of. I began to look deeply within and sort through my emotions. By understanding my inner being better I began to be able to appreciate the wonder of my physical being and, rather than seeing flaws, I saw the incredible gifts and blessings of my life that were only made possible because of my body.

I began to assemble a toolkit to help me move through life with more ease than I had ever known before. I began to be able to look in the mirror again but this time I didn't feel the sharp edges of contempt for my reflection but rather the comforting gaze from an old friend. Now, don't get me wrong... I am still learning because yoga and self-care is a practice.

You have to keep practising every single day for the love to come and, believe me when I say, it will come. I have learnt how to be wholehearted toward myself and to others. This knowledge has led me to be able to find a new way of being and the experience is so powerful that I have decided to set up my own yoga and therapy business to share this knowledge with others. So that, in time, others will know that yoga is for EVERYbody and that we are all worthy of self-love.

***

Yoga teacher, meditation guide and all-round life purpose mentor, Sarah is a wife and mum of two who loves to be in nature, finding adventure and basically wants to change the world one loving thought at a time. Sarah empowers women that feel lost in their roles and responsibilities to develop a deeper mind and body connection, to embrace the power of their authenticity and to learn that their bodies are not a barrier to a fulfilling life but rather their very own superpower.

Sarah's business is a wholehearted approach to body belief, health and well-being. Sarah knows how important it is to develop a home yoga and meditation practice along with healthy self-care routines in order to bring out the awesomeness and she wants to help you too. By learning to listen to your body and becoming your own best friend, Sarah will guide you on the journey that just may change your life forever.

If you are ready to find your brave and say yes to more adventure and joy in your life, you can connect with Sarah here:

https://sankalpayoga.co.uk
https://www.instagram.com/
sankalpayogawithsarah/
https://www.facebook.com/
sankalpayogawithsarah/

Worthless

Terri Morgan

"Come here you little bitch," he snarled, twisting his fingers in my hair and lifting my little feet off the floor, as he dragged me to 'his' chair in front of the TV. Celtic were playing again, and not doing well. So, as always, he had taken it out on my mum who was currently upstairs, black and blue from yet another of his ferocious beatings. Sitting there in silence, afraid to breathe too loudly in case I caught his attention, I couldn't stop my little body from shaking as I watched the veins pop out on his contorted face.

Our dog quivered beside me; tucking his head under my arm, he let out small whimpers each time my stepdad punched the arm of the chair. I tried to quiet him, I really did, but it was too late… I felt his stare before I even looked up. He was mad, very mad, and although I only locked eyes with him for a second, for less than a second in fact, I knew in that instant that his rampage was far from over.

You see, when mum wasn't present to receive his rage, it was often turned onto me and I just knew what was coming next. So, I did my very best to melt into the background, holding my breath as visions of what was coming flashed in my mind. He got up, stormed across the room and kicked the cowering dog who let out a pained yelp as he proceeded to drag him to the front door and throw him outside. My heart sank as I realised that there was only me left but, although my fear was making it difficult to think, my mind was filling with worry. I couldn't just leave our dog out. There was a main road in front of our house and the rain was coming down in buckets too; I feared more for his safety than my own. So, when he went to the toilet I tiptoed upstairs as quickly and quietly as I possibly could. It was even more daunting due to the fact that my legs didn't feel like my own as they shook and jellied beneath me. I told Mum what had happened and she bravely ran down the stairs, out into the pouring rain in search of my only friend. I knew I was in trouble, BIG trouble, so I just stood there in the doorway, the rain lashing at me as frosty air bit my cheeks and I waited for the inevitable.

So here we were, him in 'his' chair with me at the side being held by my hair and told repeatedly how worthless I was. That was the day I made a conscious decision to "punish" myself because I was bad. It was 1987, I was six years old, and living in constant fear became normal for me. Him taking his anger out on us, Mum trying repeatedly to escape and him finding us every time, so the cycle would start again. Mum was pregnant with my sister when she met him, so he never hurt her; classing her as his own, he showered her with love and attention. So, yet again, I just believed I was the problem and harmed myself even more. When I was seven, I stole a pound from Mum's purse. I had made my mind up and was going to my nan's. I didn't know where she lived or how to get there. We hadn't seen her for years at this point, but I believed that if I got on a bus it would take me there.

My escape plan was foiled when my mum noticed the pound was missing, and the guilt I felt for stealing overwhelmed me to a point where I just blurted out my plan. Mum's face fell as the realisation of what could have happened dawned on her, and she grabbed for me, but my fear made me step back and flinch, which only made her expression more heart-breaking. She pulled me into a tight hug, apologising over and over as she kissed my face and I felt safe, for a moment anyway.

When I was eight and my sister was three, our mum wanted to take us shopping, but he had other plans in mind. She was only permitted to go if she left one of us at home with him, which obviously scared my mum. She quickly made up the excuse that we had doctor's appointments but, as she tried to leave, he clutched my sister's arm and held it on the heater. Mum tried to stop him but he just punched her and told her, through gritted teeth, that it was her fault. This was the final straw for my mum and she went to the police before having us relocated. But all my tiny mind could think was how I had endured years of abuse yet one incident with my sister had been the tipping point?! Many things happened during the four years that she was with him but that's another story. So I'll fast forward a little. At eight I was sent to my nan's; mum was pregnant with my brother by this time, so once more I felt discarded and abandoned. It was only supposed to be for a few weeks, to give Mum a break as she was now heavily pregnant, but I ended up being there for the next four years. The self-harm had escalated from ripping clumps of my hair out to biting myself and now to laceration. There were so many instances over the following years where I was abused mentally, physically, sexually and emotionally, and every incident was just extra clarification of what I'd already been conditioned to believe. It was my fault, I was worthless, and I didn't deserve to be happy.

I started to drink in excess, take drugs and harm myself multiple times each day while purging after every meal; I felt nothing. I was raped on three separate occasions and at nineteen I entered into a relationship which would almost break me completely but, again, that, my friends, is another story. Our generation was taught to "not complain", or "self-pity", or "air our business in public". So that's exactly what I did. Going from day to day with my "happy face" painted on so nobody could see that I was completely dead inside. I dressed up, went out with friends, and portrayed myself as your average bubbly teenager so nobody knew how bad things really were inside my head. I was seen as the "strong one", the resilient one, the one who supported everybody else, so I could never allow people to see weakness.

On 7th January 2009, I went for a routine appointment and, to my great surprise, I was informed I was pregnant again. I'd had multiple miscarriages by this time, so had accepted the possibility that I may never be a mum, which, to my mind, was just more clarification of the fact that I was worthless. So, hearing the doctor say those words hit me like a brick and I fell to the floor crying. I couldn't do this again, couldn't lose another baby, and I knew only too well that something would go wrong because it always did. I was wrong and in August 2009 my baby girl came into the world, all red-faced and wrinkly, but she was the most beautiful thing I had ever seen. I didn't get the huge rush of love that I'd heard about, but what I did get was a huge moment of clarity and as this little bundle lay in my arms I vowed to always do what was best for her.

So, in December of 2009, after another of our usual arguments, my boyfriend held me down and attempted to bite my nose off. He'd already broken it a few times over the years, so this wasn't much different, but I was different now. I warned him, in no uncertain terms that if he ever laid a finger on me again it would be the last time he'd see either of us and to my surprise he never did again, but what he did do was even worse in many ways, because his words still ring in my ears at times, telling me how stupid, ugly and pointless I am. Things just kept going from bad to worse, so in 2013, after two years of begging him to leave, I finally got him out and our girl could now live in a peaceful environment. For the first time ever I began to have positive thoughts for the future and the beautiful life we were to have. I had no interest in men, or relationships, so for the next four years I focused my energy on being the best mother I could be.

Then in December of 2017, due to a variety of issues, I had a breakdown, walked out of work half-way through a lesson, and just continued to walk as I went over the various ways that I could kill myself. I'd tried it eight times already, just another thing I was hopeless at, so walking in front of a train or a bus would leave less room for error and my girl wouldn't need to know that I'd chosen it purposefully. She was the only thing keeping me alive, so the thought of her having to live with the fact her mum chose suicide plagued me day and night. I couldn't work, barely ate or slept and began hiding myself away in the house. I was so tired of everything and truly believed that my daughter would be better off without me ruining everything in her life as I had done to my own. Suicide felt like my only option to make everybody happy because if they were happy then I'd be happy, wouldn't I?

After so many years of being overlooked, let down

and abused, in every way possible, my daughter's dad telling me how I was ugly, stupid, masculine and deserving of everything that had happened in my life because it was my own fault that "trouble" followed me around, wasn't anything I didn't already know. So, I accepted it completely until my child said one sentence that would change everything. As we had a bedtime story one night in early 2018, she turned to me and asked, "Do you love my dad?" "Naturally," I said. And her reply felt like a spike being driven into my heart. She looked at me through those innocent eyes and said, "Well I don't think that he loves you because you don't treat the people you love in such horrible ways," and she was so right.

It was that moment when I realised how obvious it had been and that my beautiful baby had noticed so much, even though I had done my very best to shield her. It was at that moment I realised how deluded I had been for so long. I packed some essentials for us both, bought us one way tickets and we set off to my sister's, who now resided in a beautiful little town in south Wales. We were put into a hostel for families escaping domestic abuse and it was here that my eyes were completely opened for that first time in my life and I wasn't alone! There were ladies from all walks of life, of all ages and it wasn't long before I enrolled onto the Freedom program where these women were describing my life but with their own stories. I was completely speechless and soon discovered that the abuse towards me had been many times worse than I'd actually thought.

Over the six months that we lived in the refuge, the staff, who were there 24/7, witnessed many interactions between myself, my child and her father through calls and texts, each time supporting me and pointing out the multitude of red flags. So, for the first time in my life, I felt appreciated, protected, supported and, most of all, I felt safe. Not long after, I came across a group on Facebook, quite by accident, where people played games, made jokes and posted pics, etc., so I watched for a few weeks before plucking up the courage to join in. I took a picture, just my face, and with trembling fingers I pressed the "post" button and turned Facebook off because I couldn't bear to watch as comments came in about how awful I was. But after ten minutes, curiosity had overtaken my fear, so on I went, prepared for the worst. I was wrong again, as I realised while looking through the comments, every comment was positive and encouraging and I truly couldn't believe my eyes.

As the days turned into weeks, I took and posted more pictures, joined in with a few games and slowly began to feel something completely alien to me: confidence! When I had come to Wales I was a mere seven and a half stone, greatly underweight for my 5'7" frame, so my sister had made it her mission to fatten me up as I'd already started to gain some weight, which in itself was difficult for me to accept because I already fully believed that I was fat and disgusting. But now I had some wonderful people behind me supporting me and giving constant encouragement. Then I met them, four amazing women and one true gentleman who would go on to rewire my perspective and basically save my life. They made me see myself through their eyes, they shared their struggles and they supported and encouraged me to grow every single day. They became my people, my tribe, my soulmates and two years on we're stronger and closer than ever. We are each other's cheerleaders, jesters, confidantes and much more, and I truly couldn't be more grateful to have each of those awesome earth angels in my life.

People often ask me, "What would you change if you could go back?" and my honest answer is always the same: "I would've preferred it not to have happened but without every single step, without every trauma, without every scar, I wouldn't be who I am today and that just wouldn't do because I'm an awesome warrior, a great mother, a fiercely loyal sister and friend, and an inspiration to so many." I truly believe that I was given this life not only because I was strong enough to override it but also to show people in similar positions that absolutely everything is possible with the right support and encouragement. I was born to show people that it's okay to not be okay and that there's always a silver lining, a light at the end of the tunnel, that there's always hope, you just have to know where to look. Part of me wishes I could tell you that

I'll never hurt myself again and never have negative thoughts about myself, but I'd be lying if I did. The truth is that I have to work on it every single day with affirmations, self-love and self-compassion, but that's more than okay because I now see and understand that having a negative thought, or feeling low doesn't make me weak, it simply means that I'm human. And that, my beauties, is true power. They say knowledge is power and I couldn't agree more because without the knowledge I've gained over the last two years I'd have continued to blame and punish myself for every bad thing that ever happened! Knowledge, photography and surrounding myself with amazing people, who actually see me, was my medicine for healing and still is!

What will yours be??

Much love, Terri x

***

Born in January 1981, Terri was the second child of a family of seven from Salford, Manchester. She left school at fifteen and worked various low-paid jobs, often to help support the family income, until she settled into childcare and teaching for the next eighteen years. In 2017 a series of events led to the biggest and most dramatic choices of her life, ultimately leading to a level of deep self-love and understanding.

She currently resides in South Wales, with her

eleven-year-old daughter Isabelle and their pets Rocky, Eliza and Allen.

Facebook:
https://www.facebook.com/
groups/645206683066957/user/100000662516722
E-mail: loubou09@yahoo.co.uk
Perspective Enrichment Coach

You Can Knock Me Down, But When I Get Up You're f@@ked!

Victoria Harrington-Biddle

To get to where I have it has been a very long and twisty journey.

I never really decided on what I wanted to do but the story starts after school before my GCSE exams. Sitting on the classroom floor having stressed myself out so much that memories came back that I had blocked out, I couldn't speak, just sobbing, my best friend by my side and a teacher, both helping me get out what had happened. At age eleven the abuse started. My brother (not that I consider him to be such) decided that a way to keep me from telling my parents he was stealing my pocket money, or anything of value, was to rape me (I've never written that before as it's been too difficult). That way, if I told my parents on him he would say I'd done awful things like steal from my gran, etc., etc. It was all blackmail and lies, all to keep me quiet.

The teacher took my information and went to the

headteacher or assistant head. They called my parents and the message I got back from them was that my mum said I was a drama queen; this basically shattered our relationship. Nothing was really mentioned after this for a while. I had opened a Pandora's box and it led to taking too many paracetamol one lunchtime. A friend told a teacher and the school called an ambulance. I had to ride there with a lovely guy telling me not to close my eyes. I will never forget seeing my dad's face, red and puffy from crying on his way. I hugged him so tight and he asked me why, but I couldn't talk about it with him, I was scared that he was drinking a lot, so I spoke briefly to him about that.

After breaking down at school, the silence on the topic went on. Mum told me one Sunday that I shouldn't think it had been swept under the carpet, I was still saying this is what had happened and that it would be dealt with.

I didn't hear anything about it.

The abuse didn't end until about age fifteen-ish, but it was much less. For four years I suffered and those around me that I thought would protect and help me instead turned away from me. I have complex PTSD from all the things related to this, especially to the noise of rustling crisp packets and feeling cling film when wrapping sandwiches – he used crisp packets and cling film as protection, lots of pain right there. Those simplest of everyday items can be my undoing.

I was always grateful for any guys being kind to me.

My first serious boyfriend was manipulative and mean. He said to prove I loved him I should call him at midnight in the days of free calls at midnight on NTL, as it was in the day. The last big thing I had to do to prove I loved and wanted him was to walk three miles in the middle of the night to see him. At age fifteen, I climbed out of my bedroom window and didn't go home for six months! So I ended up stuck with him because I was grateful to be told I was his girlfriend. One night he got angry and strangled me until I blacked out. Once I woke up and went to him to make excuses (no idea why), he squeezed my face in his hand so hard that my cheeks were stuck to the squares of my braces on my teeth. I stood in the bathroom picking my skin off the squares one by one, as it was painful and bloody. Another time he held a knife to my throat because I'd said the wrong thing.

This then ended up in me being held hostage in my house until a new friend from my new job came to my house to help me get out, as I'd texted them to say he had locked me in and I couldn't get out. They helped me get out of a window and hide in bushes while they kept him away from me. Eventually the new friends were able to take me home to my mum and dad.

After this I met my ex-husband. When we got together, I think we were both grateful to be honest. Initially there were no problems, then my head was turned by a guy who was a player – I ended up cheating on my ex-husband as I was getting bored. This new guy made me feel alive like never before, like there were exciting things in life. Looking back I was blinded by the dazzle and did the wrong thing. Then I fell pregnant with my first daughter – she was my ex's by the way – unfortunately after she was born I developed postnatal depression, and my husband wasn't interested, he just didn't understand it at all and he didn't try to. He just said get a grip and sort yourself out. After a long time back on tablets I eventually felt better and I got through the tough time. We spoke about having another baby and two years after the first we welcomed our second daughter. This time I hoped to escape the clutches of PND but no, no such luck, again I spiralled into depression. I took myself to the doctor eventually as I felt suicidal. He spoke to me very kindly, he said go home, get your husband and come right back, we can help you together. My husband declined, not interested, I didn't need any help, I just needed to get a grip, apparently. So, I went back on my own, got some tablets and started the journey alone again. He was so disinterested that he got his mum to drive up to Wiltshire from Cornwall!

I only made it to the baby being nine months old before I got to my lowest point; suicidal, self-harming, not eating, unable to find anyone to talk to, I felt very much alone. I had met a lovely person a few months previously and eventually I plucked up courage to talk to them about it. The relief was huge, to get it out and listen to a rational person's response was amazing. Something just seemed right, that person became my rock. I was suicidal, sitting with razor blades, crying to this person to say I can't do it, they don't need me like this and I can't get better alone.

My husband had a problem if I wore a skirt or make up on the very occasional day I tried to feel better about myself. I wasn't allowed friends over to the house but I also wasn't allowed to go out! I flew off the rails, I went to the pub even if I wasn't drinking just to try and see old friends, he hated me and what I was doing, but he wasn't interested, so it seemed better all round if when he was home I was out. I came home five minutes before he left for work and I went out after he got home; it was like this seven days a week for a while. Like I say, I only managed to deal with it for about nine months, the day of the razor blades I spoke to my soul mate who said the girls would rather have me in their lives and well than dead. He ran three miles to sit with me while I cried, we knew there was a connection for us but he knew I was there and in trouble.

My friend offered me the chance to go and stay at the shared house they lived in if I needed to get out. Finally, I took the chance, I packed a bag and went. I told my husband I couldn't do it anymore and that it was a choice between leaving – getting well and building a future for the girls to be part of and seeing that it's possible to get through these things – or die. He wasn't fussed either way by his reaction, he just said go. I went. Eventually I got myself to a point of getting a job. I worked as much as possible, then a second job and eventually a third job in a pub. I was paying my bills in my name, contributing where I could to the shared house. Low wages didn't make life easy, but I got by, just about.

For nine months I lived in the shared house and got by, seeing the girls when I was allowed, usually only when it suited him, but that was fine, at least I saw them. I was threatened with lawyer's bills and all kinds of threats to make me sign divorce papers, so in the end I signed just to be rid of him. A side to this was that as the ex-husband's dad is an accountant, he advised him to go bankrupt because it then transferred all his debt to me as we were married. This has then for years caused me problems with getting my licenses to study accounting, problems getting a bank account, etc. Thankfully I have rebuilt myself. By this point I had moved out of the shared house and into a little flat with my rock; we had a little home together, we had virtually nothing but we had each other. There were no tiles in the shower, so we duct-taped bin bags to the walls so we could shower, no washing machine so everything was washed in the kitchen sink and rinsed in the bottom of the shower. Funny the things that stick with you! We ate only the cheapest food, we would get the sale items and pasta, etc.

We found out we were expecting a little boy after a miscarriage. We were thrilled, so pleased, we worked harder and more than ever before to get into a better position to eventually get a nicer place.

We were strong together. Our son was born and we absolutely loved it, but PND hit again. This time the midwife sat with me and my rock and helped us together. I got through it with his help and love. He joined the army to get a better career, but in basic training he tore his cruciate ligament and had to be medically discharged. We moved to the Midlands to stay with his parents after I'd stayed with mine for three months in America; we moved here, got jobs, saved our pay whilst living at home for a year, then we finally moved out to our first proper house!! The excitement was massive. I started buying and selling baby goods on eBay, the market was massive and I took full advantage of it and made additional money on the side of working. My partner was working all hours, we argued a bit but got through. After three years of working our arses off we had a daughter, and our family felt complete. We stayed in our home for a year after she was born and then moved to a quieter house, on a lovely leafy close, it was bliss. But he was working all the time and never seemed to be home and I started to spend money and feel alone; I was scared to feel this way and closed off from him. I secretly started seeing someone who paid attention, and eventually, as they do, the secret got out. He knew I was broken with the guilt of what I had done. I was broken because I thought he did not want me or care, but it turns out that was not the case. We separated for eighteen months to two years. It was hard, we couldn't not see each other, we made sure the kids were our number one focus.

By this point my ex-husband had all but disappeared, moved to a new house, changed phones, etc., got a fifteen-year-old girl pregnant (when we had our son) who was the babysitter for the girls whilst he was at work. He didn't allow me any contact. From day one she made them call her mum, she threatened me in the street that I wasn't to see them. I picked the girls up from nursery one day as arranged and I didn't realise at the time, but it was one of the last times I would see them. She said, they call me mum now not you, if I ever see you down a dark street, watch your back as you'll regret leaving him.

Cards and gifts were thrown away and then asking me for money, I gave what I could, he offered for me to go back to him whilst pregnant with my son. He said if you fall down the stairs and lose the baby you can come back so you can see the girls. Did I mention his dad gave me a job after the birth of our second daughter at his office? He was going to train me to be an accountant as none of his kids wanted to take over the business when he retired, so I was going to learn and do it instead. Obviously when my husband became an ex-husband that chance went out of the window, or so I thought.

So my rock and I had separated, we tried to ensure the kids knew we both loved them (my ex told my girls that I left them, he wouldn't listen when I said it wasn't them I left it was him, he has told them repeatedly I left them as I didn't care). We weren't very good at staying separated and my rock came and spent time with us at my home, we went on days out, we spent tea times together as much as possible. Eventually, after a long time of not being able to leave each other behind, we decided to get our act together. I realised it was him I wanted, and we moved to a new house together to make sure it was the right move. We had a wonderful couple of years there and made the decision that yes it was for ever. I can't tell you the love I have for this person, after deciding to make a lifetime go of it, we took the plunge and bought a house together.

When we moved up here, we had a conversation about me becoming an accountant. I went back to college at night to get my GCSE grade C, which I needed to get on the accountancy course, which took a year. Then I did level one of the accountancy course, then the second, then had our daughter and then did the next and last level of this particular qualification. I couldn't get a job in finance as I had no experience to speak of. I got to the point of being able to do a self-assessment, if the experience wasn't going to be possible to get then I need to get my own! My business was born!!!!!!

I did one self-assessment in year one, and I still have this original client. Each year I get new ones. I'm still working full time and doing the accounts in my spare time for people. We are now in our home six and a half years after buying it, our son has 'taken' GCSEs this year, we have a daughter in year nine, and we have started doing things to the house in preparation to one day buy a forever home. We have worked hard for a long time to now be able to buy a bottle of wine and not worry. It's not been easy or straightforward at most points; the business is okay, it's not the big practice I dreamed of but after so much uncertainty I can't bring myself to take the plunge and go full time. I have too much self-doubt and not enough belief that I can do it, but I sit here now with a stack of qualifications that I have put myself through, a business that admittedly this year has shrunk due to COVID-19 and losing clients but, as a rule, it's still going eight and a half years after it started with £30 to get registered and a letter head and logo off a friend.

One thing I wish people had is belief that they can achieve. It's not always easy, very rarely straightforward but still possible. If I can come out of the end of all this shit with my partner of nearly nineteen years, two wonderful children and two others who I saw three years ago for the first time in ten years, then you can make it too. I hope one day that my older children will want to hear my side of the story. For now, though, I have no right to plough into their lives and turn them upside down by wanting to know them. They get my phone number in each card to say if you need or want anything we love you and we are here for you, just shout. They are beautiful and I dream one day we might build something. I have tried to build a life to show them that no matter what happens YOU CAN DO WHAT YOU SET YOUR HEART TO. You can be what you want to be, whatever your dreams are you can make them come true. I would love to help anyone going through so much fuc***d up shit, if anyone ever wants to talk to someone just email me; if I could help just one person feeling stuck and alone then it's all worth it.

***

Now aged forty-one, having spent the last year in menopause, Victoria is now claiming her health back slowly, running, throwing yoga shapes, etc! Living in Leicestershire, blessed to have her partner Chris and their two smalls, big is aged seventeen and small is thirteen, she is also owned by Ted cat and a bonkers Beagle Moose.

Always looking for the next course to study and qualifications to earn, she'd love to hear from and try and help anyone who finds her story helpful.

"Please know that anyone who feels it is them against the world, you've got this! You can achieve, you can succeed, hold your head up with pride and just do you."

Get in touch on:

vic@toriasbooksltd.com
www.instgram.com/toriasbooksltd

Can You Truly Love Yourself, If You Don't Even Know Yourself?

Victoria Padmore

We all understand that to meet someone else's needs and to treat them with love we first need to understand their wants and needs. Huge brands need to know what their customers want before they create a product or service. On a friend's birthday we first need to know their likes and dislikes before we find that perfect birthday pressy. By meeting their wants and desire we show our love, appreciation and respect.

So, what about ourselves? If we don't know our own wants and desires can we really show ourselves love by building a life to meet those wants and desires?

The best relationships are when you both love yourselves as much as you love each other.

My journey actually begins with an ending. It was the ending of a relationship, of a relationship that I thought was my forever. We were the "perfect" couple, everyone thought so. Young love that looked set to last forever.

This relationship spanned three to four years of my late teens, ending when I was twenty. At the time that felt like forever. Nowadays, however, I still consider a three-year-old bra as new! It was my first love, and because of that I had romanticised our future. It felt all set in stone; finish university, move in together, get married, 2.4 kids, white picket fence, the whole breakfast cereal advert family!

Then, I fucked it up! I was solely to blame for the breakdown of the relationship. I took it all for granted, risked it all and lost.

Now looking back, I know the future I had dreamed of back then wasn't actually what would have fulfilled me, but at the time it seemed perfect. I absolutely do not wish things had turned out differently now, I just wish the way it happened had been different. When we broke up, I mourned that future more than I mourned the reality of the relationship. I felt like someone had just erased my future entirely. What made it worse was that person was me. I was angry at myself for ruining MY future.

I had everything laid out, I knew what I wanted, and I knew who I was. Losing that future also seemed to erase my identity. I looked at my life and questioned: "What now?!" I didn't know who I was anymore. My whole idea of "self" was wrapped up in that relationship, so without it I just didn't know anymore. I felt the need to get that stability back, to get that safety back and to fill the unknown future. Sitting alone and not knowing what the future holds can feel terrifying. I felt like I was just moving from one day to the next with no direction or purpose anymore.

So, I needed to "find myself"! No, I didn't go backpacking to spiritual destinations, and I didn't start journaling or therapy, I just started dating – A LOT!

That felt like my answer: when in my relationship I knew who I was, I knew what I wanted and I knew what my future held, so I thought I needed a man to create my identity again.

"Who am I? Oh, I'm (insert male's name)'s girlfriend!"

That felt like the only way that I could find me again.

The problem with this plan was the plan itself! I went looking for a relationship without knowing who I was, without knowing what I wanted in a partner and without knowing what I wanted my future to hold. I then found that I was moulded by the guy. By going into a partnership without my own set of boundaries and standards, I simply took on theirs. I also took on the image of who they wanted me to be. By not having my own identity I created one that pleased him. I sought the image of myself mirrored in his eyes. I dressed, acted and reacted exactly how he thought I should, and his approval became my validation that I was on the right path to finding me. The more he liked me, or the version of me I created, the better that version must be to everyone, right?

Initially this led to superficial, short-term dating and relationships. We couldn't really bond because how could he get to know someone who didn't really know themselves? For fear of saying something wrong I said very little. I never expressed an individual opinion, I didn't really have any. Gosh, I must have been a boring date! Trust me, I am far more opinionated now.

At this stage of my journey, the only person being abusive to me was myself. I went into relationships seeking their approval. By not having my own boundaries and without being connected to my personal wants and needs I put myself in situations that started to chip away at my core values, my self-esteem and my self-respect. Situations where internally I was screaming NO but I kept a pretty smile plastered on my face.

I had sex when I didn't actually want to, the guy wouldn't have known this at the time, so he can't be blamed.

I sat silent when discriminatory jokes were made, when illegal and immoral acts played out in front of me.

It felt wrong, it felt uncomfortable, but I pushed these feelings down because the girl I was being that month thought this was okay, because the guy she was dating did!

With each of these acts and each relationship I lost

more and more of who I was and my quest to find myself moved further and further away.

I was still probably punishing myself for losing the future I thought I so desperately wanted. By now I was so lost, so detached from my true identity that I didn't know how to get back. I continued to search with new dates.

I was so obviously a "lost soul" who was desperately seeking something, but I didn't even know what that was.

With every breakup or failed date I asked myself: "What now?!" And with each breakup the question became more desperate and the answer became further away.

Up until now the guys I dated weren't really abusive. They definitely weren't great guys and yes, they pushed my boundaries and disrespected me, but I don't think they set out to. They were just being their shitty selves, who didn't really treat anyone particularly nicely.

However, I very quickly found that the men who were very ready to help me answer my eternal "what now?!" question were men who wanted to hold the agenda. In my case men who were very ready to tell me what I wanted, what I would accept and what I could give them. These men knew what they were doing, and I was a ready-made broken soul for them to play with.

This stage of my journey is when I moved from

abusing myself in relationships with men who didn't really know what was happening, to men who were very ready to use my confusion to abuse me, men who knew exactly what was happening and knew exactly the power they held.

I even think I can pinpoint the tipping point. The point where the men I attracted knew they were crossing boundaries but didn't care. In fact, they were actively smashing these boundaries on purpose to see how much control they could gain.

I went on a date with a guy I had met at work. I worked in the leisure industry and he was a customer. We got chatting and he asked me out, no big romantic gestures, no story to make you swoon. He seemed to already know he didn't need to do this to get me. At this stage in my journey, I seemed to be an obvious target.

We arranged to meet in a McDonald's car park... yep, something I look back on and wonder if this was his way of testing. He said my house was too far to come pick me up. With a flirty hair flick, I said, "Oh, that's fine."

As I stood in the cold, dark car park I was actually excited! I still did get excited, I was still desperately searching for that true love again, trying to find the happy ever after that I thought I had lost. I just searched in the wrong places, under ever stone and rock... obviously I only found slugs and bugs. Of course, he was late. This may sound like nothing but wrapped up in everything else it was a power play, I see that now. First, he wanted to see if I would stand in a dirty car park and then he wanted to see how long I would stand in a dirty car park. You see, the girl who said no and laughed in his face or the girl who held too much self-respect to wait the hour in the car park – yes, an hour! – that girl was not his type. He needed the girl who would give a flirty hair flick and say, "Oh, that's fine."

I wanted to be the fun girl, I wanted to be the perfect girlfriend and they didn't answer back or call out bullshit, right? I also wanted this date more than I wanted my self-respect.

We went to the cinema. I don't remember much about the car ride there, I don't remember the film, I don't remember much about what he looked like, to be honest. But there are things I remember that I will never forget.

He had already made a lot of sexual comments about my body, especially my breasts, again I now think these were tests to see how far he could go. I would never accept this disrespect now. Once the film started and the lights went down, he grabbed my hands forcefully. I struggled to get free and I did. He continued this until he had a tight, painful grip on both wrists. He took one of my hands and sat on it, drawing me closer to him and making it impossible to escape, even though I tried. I struggled and used all my strength to get away. His grip loosened at times, but he always regained control. This is when he put his free hand down my top, roughly inside my bra. No words were said, no eye contact was being made. So why didn't someone else in the cinema help me? Why didn't someone stop this sexual assault happening right before them?

They didn't help because I was giggling. It was an awkward, nervous giggle but I was giggling. Inside I was screaming and crying. Inside it felt so wrong, it was painful, and I was not enjoying any of this. Outside, though, I didn't break my role of the fun girl. My self-respect was so broken that I giggled. Yes, I was saying "stop" but anyone watching on would have seen it as a playful exchange between lovers. They couldn't see how rough he was holding my wrist, they couldn't see the bruises that were forming. They couldn't see the fear in my eyes. I just kept giggling. This was my first introduction to abusive men, and I giggled my way through it. I didn't see this guy again, he didn't call, but to be honest if he had I may have even seen him again.

After he dropped me home, I locked every door twice and cried. I cried out of fear, out of embarrassment but also out of anger at myself. I, once again, blamed myself. This was a response that became habit for me and many women who experience abusive relationships, to blame themselves. In this case it started with, "Was my top too low cut?" and, "Did I invite this behaviour?" and then, "Why did I giggle?!", "Why did I LET him treat me that way?" I was so angry at myself and all night played out different scenarios of how I wish I had acted. Each time my behaviour was different and then it wouldn't have happened. Now I absolutely know the only person to blame, the only person who should be regretting their actions, was him. I was not to blame for his actions, and I wasn't strong enough to react differently. However, that was not my fault! An abusive man's behaviour is his to own.

Unfortunately, this self-hatred after the date didn't make me change my ways, in fact this incident just made me feel even less worthy and drop my boundaries even further.

So why have I chosen this event to tell you about? It was just one date. How could this play such a big role in my story? This was a huge tipping point for me, we all need to look out for points like this. This experience should have been the very point I stopped, I regained my self-respect, my self-worth and I should have promised myself I would never feel this way ever again. This should have been a very real glimpse of my future. It wasn't, though, and it go so much worse. If I had stopped at this point, the following abuse could never have happened. That does not make the following abuse my fault, absolutely not! What I am saying is that if I had regained my self-love at this point, my future relationships would have been different because I would have chosen different partners all together.

The pattern continued and the men got more abusive. With each relationship more boundaries were smashed down, my self-esteem and self-worth got worse. With each relationship ending, the question of "What now?!" got louder and the question of "Who am I?!" got more desperate.

My search for the future I wanted to live had led down a very dark path, which included financial abuse, emotional abuse, sexual abuse and physical abuse. To the point that when my ex-boyfriend's fist first connected with my jaw I wasn't even surprised.

The level of abuse got worse with each new boyfriend because I never took the time to reset between relationships, to reconnect with myself. When I looked at what I accepted in the relationship that just ended I set that to be my new standard, my new set of boundaries and each time they were lower and lower. Most stories of abuse follow this pattern that at first he was loving and caring and slowly he started to drip in evil and abuse, so slowly that you don't see it until you are so deep you are drowning. My experience was just that it happened over a string of relationships.

The end of an abusive relationship for any woman is absolutely not the end of her journey, it is always just the beginning and the risk of her jumping straight back into another abusive relationship is so high. *If you, or your friend has just come out of an abusive relationship it is now that you get to redesign your future.*

Just because you accepted something in a previous

relationship DOES NOT mean you need to accept it again. This is not your standard, it was his! Don't take him with you into your next relationship. This is also true of current relationships as well. Just because there is something you have "accepted" up until now does not mean you have to continue to accept it as your relationship continues. If he can't meet you at your standards and stay within your boundaries, then is this really going to lead to the future you want and deserve?

I only broke this cycle of abusive relationships once I stopped and remembered how to dream. I remembered how to dream of a future I wanted to live, in all aspects of life. I took time to dream of a completely different life, one that was closer to the core of who I was. I removed every single action and emotion that did not fit into the future I wanted to live. I kept this image in my mind with every single choice I made in life and soon I started to believe I not only wanted that future, but I deserved it. It took time and I had to consciously ask myself, "Does this fit with your dream future?" until I became better at making decisions that were protecting myself. Only then did I allow myself to look at a new relationship and by now my dream future was so set in my vision that he had to fit in with that. I knew what my future looked like for myself first and it absolutely did not include abuse in any way.

The question "What now?!" can only be answered

by yourself and it is far more fun to answer this yourself because then you build an image of your future that is all yours! An image that completely fulfils you and excites you! Surely that is much more fun to work towards than a future that someone else has designed and you are just playing out?

***

Following my own experiences of how daunting it is leaving an abusive relationship without knowing what is next in your life and the fear that you cannot create your own future, I founded the More to her Life charity. More to her Life supports women who have experienced domestic abuse by delivering gifts and experiences designed to give them a glimpse of how amazing life away from abuse can be and that they have the power to create this themselves.

I collaborate with inspirational people who also want to support these women and together we create impactful projects.

I would love to hear from you if you need support following an abusive relationship, if you want to support the charity or if you just need to talk. There is a contact form on the website, which I answer personally:

www.moretoherlife.co.uk